Business Guides on the Go

"Business Guides on the Go" presents cutting-edge insights from practice on particular topics within the fields of business, management, and finance. Written by practitioners and experts in a concise and accessible form the series provides professionals with a general understanding and a first practical approach to latest developments in business strategy, leadership, operations, HR management, innovation and technology management, marketing or digitalization. Students of business administration or management will also benefit from these practical guides for their future occupation/careers.

These Guides suit the needs of today's fast reader.

Marc-Felix Otto

Management of Political Risks

Fundamentals and Tools for Executives and Entrepreneurs

Marc-Felix Otto
The Advisory House AG
Zug, Switzerland

ISSN 2731-4758　　　　　　　ISSN 2731-4766　(electronic)
Business Guides on the Go
ISBN 978-3-658-42638-5　　　ISBN 978-3-658-42639-2　(eBook)
https://doi.org/10.1007/978-3-658-42639-2

Translation from the German language edition: "Politische Risiken" by Marc-Felix Otto, © Der/die Herausgeber bzw. der/die Autor(en), exklusiv lizenziert an Springer Fachmedien Wiesbaden GmbH, ein Teil von Springer Nature 2023. Published by Springer Fachmedien Wiesbaden. All Rights Reserved.

© The Editor(s) (if applicable) and The Author(s), under exclusive license to Springer Fachmedien Wiesbaden GmbH, part of Springer Nature 2023

This work is subject to copyright. All rights are solely and exclusively licensed by the Publisher, whether the whole or part of the material is concerned, specifically the rights of translation, reprinting, reuse of illustrations, recitation, broadcasting, reproduction on microfilms or in any other physical way, and transmission or information storage and retrieval, electronic adaptation, computer software, or by similar or dissimilar methodology now known or hereafter developed.

The use of general descriptive names, registered names, trademarks, service marks, etc. in this publication does not imply, even in the absence of a specific statement, that such names are exempt from the relevant protective laws and regulations and therefore free for general use.

The publisher, the authors, and the editors are safe to assume that the advice and information in this book are believed to be true and accurate at the date of publication. Neither the publisher nor the authors or the editors give a warranty, expressed or implied, with respect to the material contained herein or for any errors or omissions that may have been made. The publisher remains neutral with regard to jurisdictional claims in published maps and institutional affiliations.

This Springer imprint is published by the registered company Springer Fachmedien Wiesbaden GmbH, part of Springer Nature.
The registered company address is: Abraham-Lincoln-Str. 46, 65189 Wiesbaden, Germany

Paper in this product is recyclable.

Contents

1	**Introduction**	1
	1.1 Objective and Structure	4
	1.2 Delimitation	5
	References	6
2	**Overview of Political Risks**	7
	2.1 Definitions	8
	2.1.1 Power, Politics, State, and Jurisdiction	8
	2.1.2 Political Risks in the Narrower Sense	9
	2.1.3 Risks from Unlawful Behavior by Political Actors	10
	2.1.4 Political Changes as a Positive Value Driver	12
	2.2 Emergence of Political Risks	12
	2.3 Characteristics of Political Risks	14
	2.3.1 Different Classifications in the Literature	14
	2.3.2 Classification by Financial Value Drivers	16
	2.4 Allocating Political Risks to the Investment Portfolio	20
	2.5 Significance and Drivers of Political Risks	22
	2.5.1 Economic Significance	23
	2.5.2 Significance for a Specific Company	25
	2.5.3 Drivers of Political Risks	26
	References	31

Contents

3 Methods of General Risk Management — 33
- 3.1 Risk Identification and Description — 34
- 3.2 Risk Assessment — 38
- 3.3 Dealing with Risks — 40
  - 3.3.1 Step 1: Selecting the Course of Action — 40
  - 3.3.2 Step 2: Implementation — 43
  - 3.3.3 Step 3: Risk Control — 43
- 3.4 Embedding in Corporate Organizations — 44
- 3.5 Strategic Risk and Portfolio Management — 46
- References — 49

4 Create Transparency About Political Risks — 51
- 4.1 Identify and Describe Political Risks — 51
- 4.2 Assess Political Risks — 55
  - 4.2.1 Evaluating a Single Risk — 58
  - 4.2.2 Evaluating Multiple Risks — 62
- 4.3 Controlling and Monitoring — 69
- 4.4 Distinction Between Tactical and Strategic Risks — 73
  - 4.4.1 Differentiation Based on Impact — 74
  - 4.4.2 Differentiation Based on Strategic Importance — 74
- References — 77

5 Managing Tactical Political Risks — 79
- 5.1 Ex Ante Options for Action — 80
- 5.2 Ex Post Options for Action — 83
  - 5.2.1 Compliance — 85
  - 5.2.2 Dissuasion/Lobbying — 87
  - 5.2.3 Withdrawal — 89
- 5.3 Synthesis of the Options for Action — 90
- 5.4 Selecting the Course of Action — 92
  - 5.4.1 Selecting the Course of Action Ex Ante — 92
  - 5.4.2 Consideration of the Ex Post Options for Action — 93
- 5.5 Implementation and Operationalization — 95
  - 5.5.1 Leadership and Culture — 96
  - 5.5.2 Organizational Structure — 98

		5.5.3 Operationalization in Processes and IT	99
	References		102

6 Managing Strategic Political Risks — 103
6.1 Strategic Risks as a Real Option — 105
6.2 Strategic Competitive Advantages Versus Political Risks — 107
    6.2.1 Examine Political Risks for Potential Competitive Advantages — 107
    6.2.2 Investigate the Impact of Political Risks on Existing Competitive Advantages — 112
6.3 Strategic Portfolio Management — 117
6.4 Dealing with Risks that Endanger the Company's Existence — 119
6.5 Integration of Political Risks into the Strategic Leadership Process — 120
    6.5.1 Analysis — 121
    6.5.2 Vision, Mission Statement, Positioning — 122
    6.5.3 Strategic Goals — 122
    6.5.4 Measures — 122
    6.5.5 Implementation/Control — 123
6.6 Implementation and Operationalization — 123
    6.6.1 Leadership and Culture — 123
    6.6.2 Organizational Structure — 124
    6.6.3 Operationalization in Projects, Processes, and IT — 125
References — 128

7 Geographic Flexibility as a Key Strategy in Political Risk Management — 131
7.1 Historical and Current Context of the Geographically Flexible Company — 134
7.2 Overview of the Procedure and Decision Path — 137
    7.2.1 First Project Phase — 137
    7.2.2 Second Project Phase — 138
    7.2.3 Third Project Phase — 140
    7.2.4 Fourth and Fifth Project Phase — 141

	7.3	Geographical Flexibility of Assets	141
		7.3.1 Digitize IP and Processes	144
		7.3.2 Flexible Employees: Agile Organization, People Mobility, Work from Anywhere	146
		7.3.3 Reduce Physical Assets in the Business Model or in the Value Chain	147
		7.3.4 Deal with the Remaining Immobile Physical Assets	148
		7.3.5 Structural Flexibilization	150
	7.4	Selection of Target Jurisdictions	153
	7.5	Perspective of the Jurisdiction and Its Defensive Measures	160
	References	163
8	**Concluding Remarks**	165
	Reference	168
Appendix A: Taxonomy of Human Actions	169
Appendix B: Tool to Support Scenario Analysis	173
References	178

About the Author

Marc-Felix Otto Partner and Chairman of the Board of Directors of The Advisory House AG in Zug. PhD in Physics at the Max Planck Institute for Fluid Dynamics and Georg August University Göttingen. M.Sc. in Physics at Georgia Tech. Worked for McKinsey & Comp. for several years, most recently as Engagement Manager. Current consulting focus on the energy industry, including risk management for energy trading organizations. Publications on topics of risk management as well as economic philosophy. Member of the Board of the Free Cities Foundation.

1

Introduction

Why a book about managing political risks? The short answer is: First, because they are on the rise, sometimes even threatening the very existence of companies. Accordingly, it becomes more important to manage them professionally. Second, because new opportunities are arising regarding the handling of these risks. Those who do not use the opportunities may miss out on critical value potential. And third, because the topic has not yet been comprehensively addressed: The existing literature focuses on political investment risks in developing countries. For industrialized countries, political risks are considered only from the compliance management perspective.

Why are political risks becoming more significant? Geopolitical risks have recently come to the forefront. These risks can take on drastic proportions and endanger companies, entire industries, or even national economies. Even if the consequences are not always so severe, actions such as sanctions can substantially weaken companies with business partners in rival jurisdictions.

In addition to geopolitical drivers, increased regulation plays an important role. In the USA, for example, the volume of applicable national legislation (such as the Code of Federal Regulations) has grown steadily over the past fifty years from about 20,000 pages to now over 180,000 (Regulatory Studies, n.d.). In Switzerland, as another example, legislative activity is steadily increasing; the annual volume of new regulatory code is now almost 40% higher than in 1980 (Parlament, n.d.). This does not even consider the cumulative effect of adding to existing legislation. Such a development has definite consequences for companies. According to a study by the consulting firm McKinsey, the costs of regulatory risk management for banks increased by about 40% in the period from 2014–2017 alone (Mckinsey, n.d.).

Other prominent indicators of political risk are sovereign debt and inflation. Sovereign debt is well above 60% of gross domestic product in many Western countries. Highly indebted entities tend to focus more on the short term, often exhibiting erratic and radical behavior. In recent decades, vital deflationary drivers such as globalization and digitization have compensated for the inflationary effects of rising public debt, yielding overall stable consumer prices. More recently, with stagnating or declining globalization, inflation has been rising in many countries.

Finally, in the World Economic Forum's Global Risk Report, the risk of eroding social cohesion shows the largest increase of all risks recorded during the Covid years. In many countries, the way that governments dealt with the situation directly threatened many companies' existence. In conclusion, it is assumed that political risks will continue to increase or at least remain at the current high level.

What opportunities arise in connection with these risks? Besides the classic approach of avoiding or reducing risks, there may be options to create a competitive advantage. One option aims at influencing the political actors. Such lobbying has been well-known for many decades and has been increasing, especially since the 2008 financial crisis, apparently with success. For example, the Strategas agency has defined a lobbying index of publicly traded companies that includes the leaders in terms of effort spent on influencing policy. This index has systematically beaten the S&P 500 index for a long time (Barrons, n.d.). A look at Europe shows that the number of high-level meetings between EU Commission officials and company representatives has doubled over the period from 2012–2018 (Welt, n.d.; FAZ, n.d.).

On another level, political upheaval may improve the market position of companies that exhibit a high level of resilience. Resilience can be strengthened locally, for example by a culture and values that promise reliability and security to employees, suppliers, and customers. Specific redundancies, such as additional inventories of critical semi-finished goods or an additional data backup layer, can increase resilience on a regional or global level.

Another fundamental option for dealing with political risks is to make the company more geographically flexible and thus less dependent on its current location. A company with a high degree of geographic flexibility can select the most suitable jurisdictions and develop a significant advantage over competitors. This applies to the location of individual corporate functions as well as the headquarters. Digitization creates new ways to achieve this goal. In the service and knowledge sector in particular, geographic flexibility is often easy to implement—but other companies can benefit as well.

Some companies have already implemented active, strategic political risk management. Others, especially those in the "new economy," have even been established on this basis. The first step is to understand the company as an independent institution, not as subordinate to the current home state. The relationship with the jurisdiction is then on the same level as the relationships with suppliers, service providers, and customers.

In a sense, geographic flexibility continues the trend of globalization at a time when international supply chain vulnerabilities have become more apparent. In recent decades, the share of international companies in global value creation has steadily increased. This puts pressure on corporate tax rates and, in some cases, reduces market intervention in multiple jurisdictions. This trend may now be reversing. The current geopolitical crisis surrounding the Ukraine war and tensions off the coast of China are causing economic unbundling and a return to more regional, redundant value chains. Additionally, jurisdictions undertake increased efforts to reduce tax competition. Importantly, the OECD's Base Erosion and Profit Shifting (BEPS) initiative has been formulated as a response to digitization. Another example is the tightening of German exit taxation. Ultimately, such political developments have an impact on the options for managing political risks. Nonetheless, with new complexities come new opportunities as well.

Companies that closely follow these trends and leverage them can significantly reduce their exposure and add value. Rapid, effective use of new technology and holistic consideration of options for alternative jurisdictions play an essential role.

How has the topic been addressed so far? Comprehensive political risk management in industrialized countries has not been adequately treated yet. Rather, since the 1980s, literature has focused on risks in developing countries. While this focus may be narrow, we can build on the risk categories developed there. We can also employ the various established methods of general risk management. From these starting points, we develop a comprehensive approach to dealing with tactical and strategic political risks. However, we focus not only on the concept. Rather, this book aims to give owners, decision-makers, and risk managers practical options for action and implementation. This purpose is served by illustrative examples and tools as well as references to further literature and knowledge sources.

1.1 Objective and Structure

The basic task of managing political risks is to avert or limit their negative impact on enterprise value. This book aims to sensitize corporate decision-makers to political risks, to give them the tools they need to deal with them, and to show them strategic options about how their company can create value in connection with the risks.

In a broader sense, it can also be read as a guide about how to handle personal or individual political risks. When interpreted this way, some aspects, like the optimal organizational structure, become irrelevant. However, the basic approach and method still apply.

At the basic level, the book is divided into two parts: In the first part, we define and categorize political risks (Chap. 2) and introduce essential general risk management methods (Chap. 3). We then discuss how to create transparency on the risks affecting the company. This includes both risk identification and evaluation (Chap. 4).

The second part focuses on dealing with political risks in practice. In Chap. 5, tactical political risk management is presented. Chapter 6 answers the question of how to deal with political risks from a strategic perspective. Chapter 7 then delves into an important option of strategic political risk management, the geographic flexibility of the company. Chapter 8 contains a short synthesis of the essential methods and shows possible fields to expand the discipline.

The concepts and methods are illustrated by three practical examples. While these are not actual real-life examples, they are based on the experience of the author and his company. They are introduced in Chap. 4 and continually elaborated on from there (Fig. 1.1).

1.2 Delimitation

This book does not intend to address the topic from every conceivable angle. The perspective we adopt is the viewpoint of entrepreneurs or business leaders who act independently and do not consider themselves as a part of public institutions. We also devote only a small amount of attention to a sub-aspect that has already been widely studied, the specific risks to foreign investment by multinational corporations. In Sect. 2.1.3, we briefly discuss this special topic and list several references.

Furthermore, we treat corporate governance as a single entity and assume that there are no conflicting objectives between owners and executives. In other words, we assume that the principal and agent are congruent at the top level of corporate management. Accordingly, we do not understand risk management as a formal bureaucratic requirement, but as a value-adding function that can significantly influence corporate strategy and success. Consequently, we only provide a basic discussion of risk management standards such as ISO or COSO ERM.

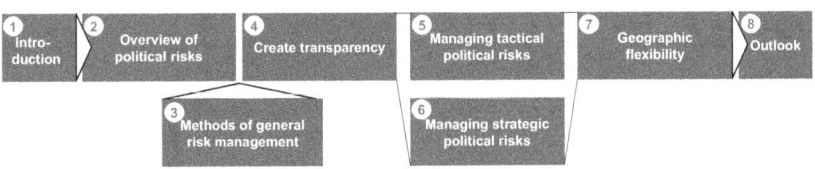

Fig. 1.1 Chapter structure

References

Barrons. (n.d.). https://www.barrons.com/articles/lobbying-index-beats-the-market-1524863200

FAZ. (n.d.). https://www.faz.net/aktuell/wirtschaft/schneller-schlau/lobbyismus-in-europa-auf-rekordniveau-15852363.html

Mckinsey. (n.d.). https://www.mckinsey.com/capabilities/risk-and-resilience/our-insights/the-compliance-function-at-an-inflection-point

Parlament. (n.d.). https://www.parlament.ch/centers/documents/de/gesetzgebungstaetigkeit-1983-2007.pdf

Regulatory Studies. (n.d.). https://regulatorystudies.columbian.gwu.edu/reg-stats

Welt. (n.d.). https://www.welt.de/wirtschaft/article132847664/Wie-der-Finanzmarkt-Lobbyismus-belohnt.html

2

Overview of Political Risks

The term political risk was coined in the Anglo-Saxon sphere in the second half of the last century. Although the term appears to be broad, the focus was and still is primarily on risks to foreign direct investment (FDI) in developing countries and emerging markets. For an overview, see (Weimer, 2000) or (Giambona et al., 2017). By contrast, evolving rules of the game in industrialized countries are often included under the term regulatory risk. We hold that this kind of distinction is no more appropriate in the globalized economy.

We start in Sect. 2.1 with a comprehensive definition of political risks. The fact that politics can unilaterally change the rules of the game is essential. By contrast, activities of political actors that conflict with applicable law do not usually fall under the concept of "politics." Hence, risks arising from this should not be referred to as political risks.

Politically charged issues often provoke partisan and emotional spokespeople. Differentiated, polarized discourse in the digital age often reinforces positions. We pursue a neutral, fact-oriented approach. The goal is to help corporate decision-makers more easily identify and assess political risks and to avert or at least reduce the damage they threaten to cause to the company. It is obvious that this can lead to corporate strategies that are not in the interests of some political players. An unbiased observer will easily recognize the side of the debate where value creation is endorsed. Accordingly, in Sect. 2.2, we also address the ethical and normative dimension of the issue.

In accordance with our objective, we structure political risks in Sect. 2.3 with the financial value drivers of the company in mind. For the sake of completeness, we also present alternative structures or classifications that may be useful in practice. The description of political risks relating to financial value drivers can be used to describe companies as a portfolio of investments with different risks. We briefly present this approach in Sect. 2.4. In Sect. 2.5, we examine the scope and likelihood of certain political risks from a general perspective.

2.1 Definitions

2.1.1 Power, Politics, State, and Jurisdiction

In order to obtain a definition of political risks, we need to clarify some basic social science concepts. This book is not intended to give a holistic approach. That is why we draw on classical works that are still valid and useful today. We refer to Max Weber to define the concept of *power* as "the probability that one actor within a social relationship will be in a position to carry out his own will despite resistance, regardless of the basis on which this probability rests" (Weber, 1921). Politics, again according to Weber, are then "striving for a share of power or for influence on the distribution of power" (Weber, 1992). Alternatively, Machiavelli formulates that "politics are the sum of the means necessary to come to power, to hold on to power, and to make the most useful use of power" (Pfetsch, 2003).

Max Weber sees the *state* as "a human community that successfully claims the monopoly of the legitimate use of physical force within a given territory" (Weber, 1972). In this context, the state or territorial entity typically consists of the three elements of the legislative, executive, and judicial branches.

In this book, we often use the term *jurisdiction*, which is sometimes also used to refer to the third branch of the state.[1] More recently, this term has also been used synonymously with "territory," that is, the territory where a particular legal code applies and is generally enforced. In this sense, the term is well suited for our purposes because it also includes subordinate territorial authorities such as the federal state or municipal authorities, which may well be a source of risks.

2.1.2 Political Risks in the Narrower Sense

Risks are possible future events with a damaging effect. Political risks in a broader sense are possible future events with a damaging effect related to politics. In industrialized countries, these are mainly events resulting from lawful behavior of political actors, typically by enacting and enforcing laws or regulations with a negative impact. Corruption that is harmful to the company, such as illegal behavior by individual political actors, is less important to us. We will nevertheless briefly discuss this in Sect. 2.1.3 below.

> **Definition**
> We define political risks in the *narrower sense* as possible future actions by the state or local authority or jurisdiction, which, if taken, will harm the company in question. In this context, harm means a reduction of enterprise value.

As listed above, state and regional authorities as well as jurisdictions can be divided into the three functional elements of the legislative, executive, and judicial branches. This clarifies how the concept is different from the concept of regulatory risks:[2] These risks exclusively cover events where the company is harmed as a result of changing legislation.

---

[1] We use the unambiguous term "judiciary" for the judicial branch throughout.
[2] Also "compliance risks"; in our view, this is a poor term because it contains a specific, potential course of action ("compliance"). The fact that compliance is by no means the only possible action and not always the optimal one is explained in Chap. 5.

Consequently, they can also be referred to as "legislative risks". However, the method of enforcement is largely the responsibility of the executive branch, as illustrated by the distinction between "de jure" and "de facto". Finally, for de facto enforcement, the judiciary has discretionary powers to enforce the law.

Political risks according to our definition therefore include legislative (regulatory), executive, and judicial risks. This distinction is not always essential for the company, but it can help estimate the speed or likelihood of a risk event: For example, legislative changes tend to take more time than executive decisions. We will come back to this in the political risk assessment.

When defining political risks from a company's perspective, it is important to distinguish between political rules and practices that already existed at the time the company was founded and those that will be added or changed at a later date. Only those that are added or changed later can constitute a risk, namely a possible future event with a negative impact. In other words, every company is deliberately founded in a specific political context. Only a deterioration of this context compared with the time when the company was founded (special case: when it moved into the jurisdiction) constitutes a materialized political risk. This definition clearly extends the classical notion of political risk, which focused on investment risks in developing countries (Sottilotta, 2016; Weimer, 2000). Such a narrow definition was not necessary because it is obvious that political risks have always played a significant role in industrialized countries as well.

2.1.3 Risks from Unlawful Behavior by Political Actors

The term "sovereign risk" is sometimes also used for political risks as defined in the last section above (Corsetti et al., 2013). In the literature, the possible damage due to specific activities of political actors is referred to as "non-sovereign risk" if these actors act in violation of the law (Stephens, 1999). An example might be a mayor illegally blackmailing a local shop to enforce support for his political campaign.

We recognize that the boundary between sovereign and non-sovereign risk can become blurred when there are weak institutions or a lack of social consensus. For several reasons, however, we do not extend our notion of political risk but deliberately exclude illegal acts by political actors: First, it is unclear whether actors who break the law are really acting out of political motives or merely pretending to do so. Second, as in the above example, such activities typically cross the line into *crime* and *corruption*. Third, dealing with such risks is fundamentally different since the company can often make use of the rule of law to avert the non-sovereign risk.

Figure 2.1 illustrates the resulting definitions of political risks.

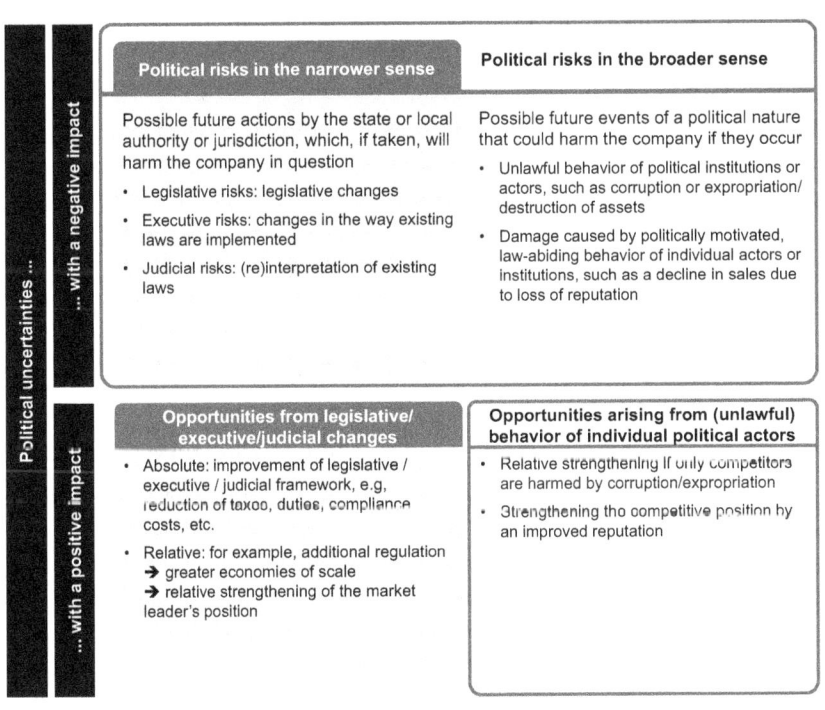

Fig. 2.1 Comparison of different definitions of political risks

2.1.4 Political Changes as a Positive Value Driver

The concept of risk implies uncertainty. This can also have positive effects on the company: Legislative, executive, or judicial changes can improve the company's situation both in *absolute terms* and *relative to competitors* *(Weimer, 2000)*.

An absolute improvement can come from reducing regulations, taxes, etc. that hinder business. A key example for such an improvement in the history of the Federal Republic of Germany is when Ludwig Erhard abolished state price controls in 1948. This was a prerequisite for Germany's strong economic growth in the following decades. At that time, Erhard's decision was quite surprising and constituted a short-term disadvantage for some market participants.

A relative improvement exists if the company can take advantage of changes to the rules of the game. For example, additional regulation can increase barriers to competition or strengthen economies of scale. Large, market-leading companies often benefit from this. Additional data protection requirements, for example, indirectly squeeze out smaller information platforms and thus strengthen the virtual monopoly position of the large platforms. These market leaders, however, may bear higher risks under antitrust law and thereby suffer a relative disadvantage to smaller competitors.

The opportunities to derive strategic benefits from risks are the focus of strategic risk management. We address the topic in Chaps. 6 and 7.

2.2 Emergence of Political Risks

How do political risks occur? To answer this question, we first examine how political risks relate to other categories of risk. At a basic level, we can distinguish between man-made risks and natural risks. Natural risks, as well as risks from unintentional actions such as occupational or traffic accidents, can be studied statistically, given sufficient data. Man-made risks can be the result of intentional or unintentional actions.

Political risks result from intentional human actions and, like human free will in general, cannot be examined by statistics. If we assume that actors are rational, however, incentives can be studied to explain or predict their actions. This is the goal of public choice theory (Buchanan & Tullock, 2003). More recently, societal simulations have been used to explain or predict political risks. (Bharathy & Silverman, 2012) Attempts have also been made to describe the political strategy of "unpredictability" (Lerner, n.d.).

Monti-Belkaoui et al. (Weimer, 2000) list five other explanatory approaches in addition to such actor-based theories:

- Relative deprivation approach: The explanation that the jurisdiction or its resident population feels disadvantaged compared to the company, resulting in political instability.
- Product/venture approach: The study of which products or activities are specifically affected by political risks. In our view, this is a categorization and not an explanatory approach.
- Structural approach: The same for specific industries, organizations, or projects.
- Bargaining power approach: The study of how a company's bargaining power is represented in the jurisdiction.
- Government-type approach: The study of which forms of government are vulnerable to particular political risks.

Moreover, the emergence of political risks can be explained based on a fundamental analysis of intentional human actions. We address this in Appendix A. From such a perspective, political actions use the threat of sanctions to induce citizens and firms to behave in certain ways. A commonplace example is the penalty for avoiding tax payments, i.e., tax evasion or fraud.

This form of human interaction is not limited to political actors. Rather, threat-based or *cratic* actions are available to any people. For political actors, however, they enjoy a very high effectiveness or success rate due to the state's monopoly on the use of force. Cratic actions, therefore, are today's standard mode of governance. Political risks thus arise simply from the fact that people and human institutions can achieve their goals using threats. We regard this approach as vital to explaining how political risks occur.

Rousseau (1762) tried to invalidate the ethically questionable fact that the state system is based on threats with his postulate of a "social contract" (Rousseau, 2017). However, Gebel (2018) points out that a contract is defined as an agreement between two or more parties that cannot be changed unilaterally, by only one party. The legal code of contemporary states is continuously changed and, accordingly, cannot be a treaty. This is equally true for constitutions, even if the frequency of constitutional changes is lower. A jurisdiction, on the other hand, which interacts with its citizens based on an explicit contract that cannot be unilaterally changed would offer minimal internal political risks (Gebel, 2018). From this perspective, considering jurisdictions as a counterparty to the company, the question of relative bargaining power arises. We will revisit this question in Sect. 5.2.

Now that we have defined political risks and discussed how they occur, we will undertake to examine them in more detail.

2.3 Characteristics of Political Risks

For political risk classification, one can refer to the literature regarding investment risks in developing countries. Here, we delve into the classification based on a company's value drivers, which is a particularly suitable system for subsequent risk assessment.

2.3.1 Different Classifications in the Literature

The classifications used in the literature can be condensed to a total of four different classification methods (Weimer, 2000; McKellar, 2017; Schulze, 2009; Moran & West, 2005), see Fig. 2.2:

1. Classification by what is called *specificity of* the risk, i.e., the question of whether the risk (i) exclusively affects the company itself, (ii) the sector or industry in which the company operates, or (iii) the entire economy. An example of the entire economy being affected would be currency fluctuations caused by politics; for the second group, industry-specific regulations; and a company-specific risk would be the risk of expropriation due to political unpopularity (see Fig. 2.3).

2 Overview of Political Risks

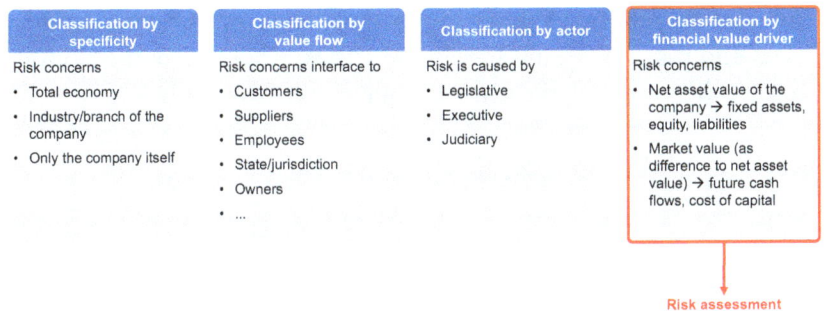

Fig. 2.2 Overview of different classifications of political risks

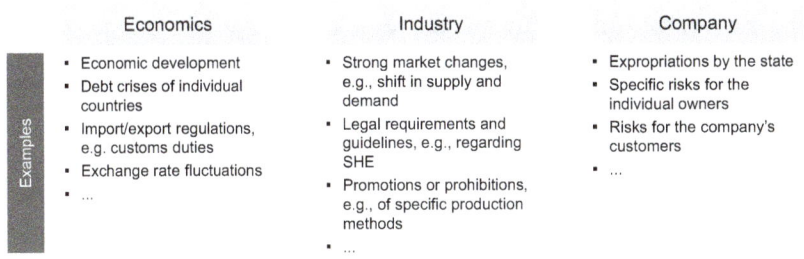

Fig. 2.3 Classification by specificity

2. Classification according to the *value flow* or contractual relationship affected by the risk. For example, the relationships with customers (increase in VAT or customs duties, ban on deliveries to certain regions, tightening of product liability, etc.), suppliers (same examples as "customers"), employees (changes in labor law, increased levies, etc.), the owners (increase in dividend tax, requirements regarding owner transparency, etc.) or the state or one of its subordinate local authorities (profit taxes, etc.).
3. Classification by *actor*, namely, the risks caused by the legislative, executive, or judicial branches.
4. Classification according to the *financial value drivers* of the company, which we will discuss in more detail in the following section. We use the term value driver in the financial sense for the sake of simplicity and for quantification purposes. A classification according to the drivers of competitive advantage is also possible. However, the method we

use has the advantage that it can be applied to practically all companies and that it does not have to be revised when the business model or the drivers of a company's strategic success change.

2.3.2 Classification by Financial Value Drivers

When we classify political risks by financial value drivers, we recall the definition of political risks: they are possible future actions of the state or local authority which reduce the enterprise value if they are carried out. This is why we examine possible types of risk related to the balance sheet and income statement of the company, in terms of what determines enterprise value. The balance sheet leads to the net asset value or book value.[3] The income statement and the cost of capital drive future discounted cash flows and thus the fair value or market value.[4] In Fig. 2.4,

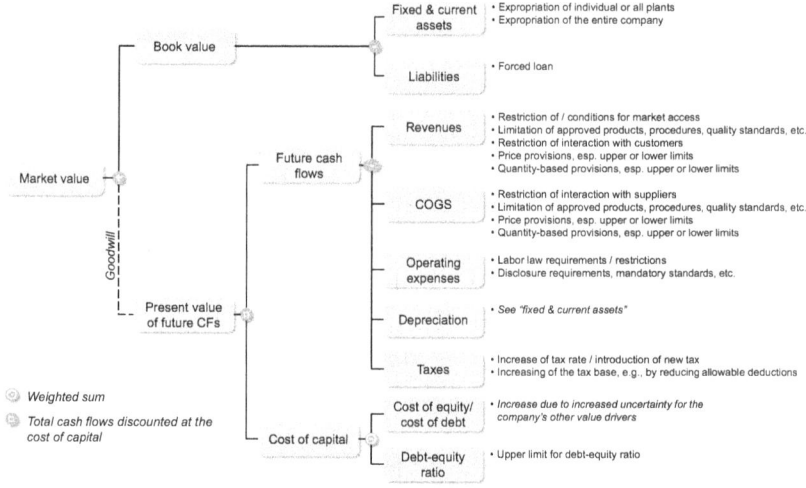

Fig. 2.4 Classification of political risks by financial value drivers

---

[3] Without considering any goodwill/market value markup.
[4] Strictly speaking, this is the cash flow. For our purposes, however, period-related effects play a less significant role, which is why we prefer the more familiar terms from the income statement.

we assign political risks to the accounting items whose value may be adversely affected.

In the following, we will expand on these risk examples and consider the dimensions "specificity," "corporate interfaces," and "actor." In other words, we point out

(a) which interface the risk typically affects: customers, suppliers, employees, or the state directly,
(b) whether the risk typically affects the entire economy, a specific sector/industry, or a specific company, and
(c) whether the risk is typically caused by the legislative or executive branch.

Book Value

Risks affecting the book value of the company have a fundamental impact. They typically occur in countries or scenarios in which societal stability is critically impaired. Roughly speaking, this involves partial or complete expropriation as well as forced loans or mortgages. If we examine possible risk types according to the top items of the balance sheet, the examination results in the following Table 2.1:

Table 2.1 Political risks regarding book value

Item	Impact on the item	Possible incident	Specificity	Interface	Actor
Fixed assets	Reduction	Expropriation of specific or all assets	Company; industry/sector	State	Legislative/Executive
Liabilities	Increase	Forced loan	Company; industry/sector; national economy	State	Legislative/Executive
Equity	Transfer	Expropriation	Company; industry/sector	State	Legislative/Executive

Market Value 1: Future Cash Flows

In line with the classic net present value method, we break down the company's market value into the two elements of future cash flows and the cost of capital. Impairments of future cash flows are perceived as less drastic than reductions in net asset value. In developed, stable economies, this is by far the predominant option, which occurs in a wide variety of ways.

The following table provides an illustrative overview; further specific risk types are possible. For the sake of simplicity, we will work with the income statement, from which the cash flow statement can be derived (Table 2.2).

Table 2.2 Political risks related to future cash flows

Item	Impact on the item	Possible incident	Specificity	Interface	Actor
Revenues	Reduction	Restriction of, or conditions for general market access (domestic/foreign)	Industry/sector; economy	Customer	Legislative
		Restriction of approved products, procedures, quality standards, etc.			
		Restriction or limitation of interaction with customers (domestic/foreign)			
		Price-related provisions, esp. maximum or minimum prices (upper or lower limits)			
		Quantity-related provisions, esp. upper or lower limits			
		Increase in value-added tax: depending on price elasticity, reduction of demand (also relevant to COGS)			

(continued)

Table 2.2 (continued)

Item	Impact on the item	Possible incident	Specificity	Interface	Actor
Cost of goods sold (COGS)	Increase	Restriction of, or conditions for interaction with suppliers (domestic/foreign)	Industry/sector; economy	Supplier	Legislative
		Restriction of approved products, procedures, quality standards, etc.			
		Price-related provisions, esp. upper or lower limits			
		Quantity-related provisions, esp. upper or lower limits			
Operating expenses (OpEx)	Increase	Additional labor law requirements, e.g., tighter protection against dismissal	Industry/sector; economy	Employees	Legislative
		Increase in social security contributions			
		Introduction/increase of minimum wages			
	Increase	Tighter compliance and transparency requirements, e.g., new disclosure requirements, regulatory reporting, etc.	Industry/sector; economy	State	Legislative
Interest	Increase	See next section "Cost of capital"	Industry/sector; economy	State	Legislative
Taxes	Increase	Increase in profit taxes	National economy	State	Legislative

Market Value 2: Cost of Capital

Usually, the company's cost of capital is only indirectly affected by political incidents. Nevertheless, these events can have significant effects, in the short term as well as in the long term.

The following table again illustrates the most important types of risk. Further specific risks are conceivable (Table 2.3).

In summary, we assess the three risk classes resulting from the classification based on the financial value drivers as follows:

- Risks relating to book value are fundamental in nature and typically occur in political crisis situations and unstable states.
- Risks concerning future cash flows are mostly caused by legislation, can have mild to drastically severe effects, and can occur in all situations and jurisdictions.
- Risks relating to the cost of capital are mostly driven indirectly by an increase in general uncertainties, except for the "risk-free rate," which in turn is significantly influenced by central bank policies.

For illustration purposes, we assign in Fig. 2.5 the examples of political risks to the other categorizations and estimate how frequent or typical a particular risk is.

2.4 Allocating Political Risks to the Investment Portfolio

The classification of political risks by financial value drivers forms the basis for quantifying these risks. This also facilitates the task of choosing the optimal course of action.

From another perspective, political risks can also be allocated to a *company's investments*. We use this form of allocation in Sect. 6.3 where it forms the basis for strategic portfolio management. To do this, the company is virtually divided into disjoint parts. This can be thought of as a "virtual filleting," i.e., as an imaginary dissection of the company to sell

Table 2.3 Political risks regarding the cost of capital

Item	Impact on the position	Possible incident	Specificity	Interface	Actor
Cost of debt	Increase	Increase in central bank interest rates ("risk-free rate")	National economy	Third-party capital providers	Executive/ Central bank
		Indirect: increase in general economic uncertainties and thus in interest rates	National economy; industry/ sector		Executive/ Legislative
Cost of equity (shareholder expectations)	Increase	Indirect: general increase of economic uncertainties and thus in expected return on equity	National economy; industry/ sector	Owner-operator	Executive/ Legislative
Debt to equity ratio	Upper limit	Regulation of maximum debt to equity ratio (e.g., for banks)	Industry/ sector	State	Legislative

the individual parts. Other possible business activities which are not yet operational are recorded as potential investments. Instead of investments, we can also speak of the elements in a company's strategic portfolio. The filleting can be done using business areas, geographies, products, technologies, and other dimensions. It is essential that the filleting is theoretically possible. Components of the company that cannot be separated like this should not be treated as elements of the investment portfolio either.

Our objective is now to divide the company in a manner that allows us to allocate the political risks as unequivocally as possible to the strategic

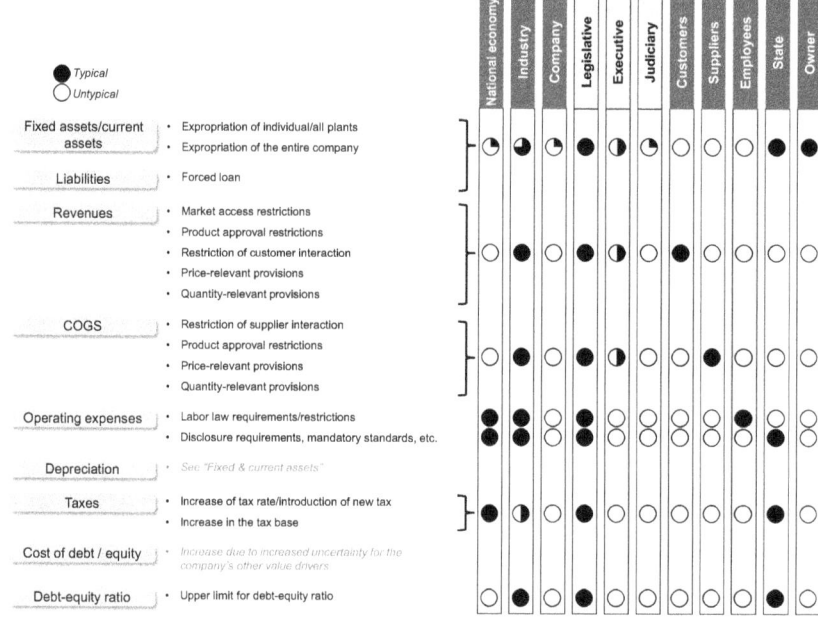

Fig. 2.5 Allocation of financial value driver risks to other dimensions

elements or investments. In other words, as few risks as possible should affect more than one element. For some types of risk, such as an increase in the profit tax rate, this will not work. In this case, the risk can be allocated proportionately to the strategic elements using a ratio. Other risks, however, can be clearly allocated, such as risks concerning the approval of specific technologies or production processes.

In the following, we outline whether and how the risk categories can be allocated to the strategic elements of a company (Table 2.4).

2.5 Significance and Drivers of Political Risks

In this section, we attempt to assess the significance of political risks. We consider this both from an economic and a business perspective. Finally, we examine the drivers of political risks.

Table 2.4 Allocation of risks to the investment portfolio

Item	Possible incident	Feasibility of allocation (typically)
Fixed assets	Expropriation of individual or all assets of the company	Allocation to individual assets → direct allocation to strategic elements possible
Liabilities/ equity	Mandatory loans; expropriation	Indirect allocation, e.g., pro rata capital
Revenues/ COGS	Restrictions; price or quantity-based regulations; increase in value-added tax.	Mostly directly attributable to strategic elements, e.g., to product groups or customer segments
Operating expenses	Tightening labor law; compliance requirements, etc.	Indirect allocation, e.g., pro rata costs
Interest/taxes/ cost of capital	Increase of cost rates	Indirect allocation, e.g., pro rata capital

2.5.1 Economic Significance

The discipline of economics is characterized by the challenge of describing complex interactions of a huge number of economic agents. What is studied is always unique in space and time. For example, different political situations cannot be used or observed in the same country at the same time. Today's good data availability allows broad empirical studies, such as a meta-study on the economic impact of political risks in (Yi et al., 2020). However, it is always possible that the observed correlations are not caused by the assumed causality but by another, unsuspected one.

We limit our analysis to a rough estimate of the economic significance of political risks based on typical economic indicators and will not dive into specific industries or companies. That would go beyond the scope of this book.

The well-known country risk serves as such an indicator. Wikipedia offers the following definition of country risk (Wikipedia, n.d.):

> **Definition**
>
> **Country risk** refers to the risk of investing or lending in a country, arising from possible changes in the business environment that may adversely affect operating profits or the value of assets in the country. For example, financial factors such as currency controls, devaluation or regulatory changes, or stability factors such as mass riots, civil war, and other potential events contribute to the company's operational risks. This term is also sometimes referred to as political risk; however, country risk is a more general term that generally refers only to risks influencing all companies operating within or involved with a particular country.

Accordingly, country risks are not exclusively composed of political risks, but also of risks caused by non-governmental counterparties in each country. However, assuming that such risks are insured by the judiciary in a well-functioning state (e.g., that a defaulting debtor is effectively ordered to pay by the court), such cases can be described as an "indirect" political risk. This view is consistent with states' claims to the monopoly on the use of force in their territories. Bekaert et al. (2014) present a method to systematically filter out non-political factors from country risks (Bekaert et al., 2014).

Country risks are regularly assessed by various institutions, e.g., by major banks or in the International Country Risk Guide (ICRG), which analyzes a total of 12 risk components monthly (PRS Group, n.d.):

- Government Stability (max. 12 points)
- Socioeconomic Conditions (max. 12 points)
- Investment Profile (max. 12 points)
- Internal Conflicts (max. 12 points)
- External Conflicts (max. 12 points)
- Corruption (max. 6 points)
- Military in politics (max. 6 points)
- Religious Tensions (max. 6 points)
- Law and order (max. 6 points)
- Ethnic Tensions (max. 6 points)
- Democratic Accountability (max. 6 points)
- Bureaucracy Quality (max. 4 points)

The maximum value of 100 points represents the minimum country risk.

In developing countries, these risks correlate with expected returns for a basket of leading equity securities (Harvey, 2004). In developed countries, this correlation is weak to non-existent, possibly because an investor can diversify the risk on the capital market (Bekaert & Harvey, 2000). However, this situation exists only for highly fungible securities and not for investments with low fungibility. Therefore, country risk can be expected to correlate with the cost of capital for low-fungibility investments. In effect, country risk is often used as an indicator of the country-specific cost of capital.

According to Harvey's analysis, a deterioration in the ICRG Composite Index by 20% of the maximum value of 100 points—i.e., by 20 absolute points—corresponds to a 5% increase in the average country-wide cost of capital. A 20% deterioration can be achieved, for example, in the "annual growth of gross domestic product" category by reducing annual growth from 2% to 0%. Other categories may react less sensitively to typical fluctuations.

> **Important**
>
> We maintain that political risks can have a drastic impact on an economy and represent a major—in many cases, the dominant—risk factor.

Consequently, political risks cannot be neglected by responsible entrepreneurs and managers. In many cases, they will even have strategic relevance.

2.5.2 Significance for a Specific Company

While the negative impact of political risks on the whole economy can hardly be doubted, the question of the specific damage to businesses caused by a particular political measure is often the subject of political debates. We do not claim to reflect all the possible or popular viewpoints.

A wide-ranging analysis of risk impact is complicated by the fact that the companies in question can react to the materialization of a political risk, which, of course, is the main topic of this book. In many cases, the damage that would be incurred by companies if they did not act can be reduced or even eliminated. When broadly analyzing enterprise values before and after the risk materializes one cannot control the effect of these reactions.

As a rule, companies themselves are best able to specifically analyze the risk impact. Outsiders with a detailed view of the business model, the value flows and the company's decision-makers might also carry out such a specific analysis, e.g., in the form of an analyst report. We discuss the appropriate valuation method from the company's perspective in Sect. 4.2.

Ultimately, the economic impact of political risks discussed above corresponds to the sum of the positive and negative effects on all the affected economic entities. It is obvious that a specific incident will affect certain industries or individual companies to different degrees. For example, a change in the law may result in insolvency for some companies, while others may benefit.

2.5.3 Drivers of Political Risks

In this section, we discuss the overarching drivers of political risk in jurisdictions. This analysis builds on the above analysis regarding the economic significance of political risks. An understanding of the risk drivers can facilitate the assessment of the risk likelihood, which we examine in Sect. 4.2.

We distinguish between the two main groups of counterparties for a specific jurisdiction: the "domestic" group of residents, voters, taxpayers, etc. and the "foreign" group of other jurisdictions, whether they are allied, rivalling, or neutral.

The following consideration is a qualitative one; quantifying the likelihood at the macroeconomic level would require further work, as we discuss in Chap. 8.

Domestic Drivers

Domestically, most jurisdictions face significantly inferior counterparties, both militarily and economically. However, the problem of legitimacy (or consent, support, identification) remains, which is very relevant for the long-term success of jurisdictions and their representatives. Legitimacy, in turn, is influenced by a variety of factors that can be roughly divided into economic and moral or cultural ones. The latter may be difficult to quantify but are by no means less important than economic factors.

Shapiro specifically examines the drivers of political risk in developing countries (Shapiro, 1985). In particular, he mentions the following drivers:

- High public debt, measured in debt/GDP
- High growth of the money supply, coupled with a fixed exchange rate to the currency of a developed country
- High government spending with low economic impact
- Price controls, interest rate caps, trade restrictions and other constraints on price discovery
- An expectation by the people—supported by politicians—aimed at raising the standard of living through government benefits

For industrialized countries, we first analyze the correlation of economic performance with different possible risk drivers based on country data from the Global Economy (https://www.theglobaleconomy.com/, n.d.). We focus on countries with a Human Development Index (HDI) value above 0.8 ("high") and relative dominance of Catholic or Protestant Christianity, in order to adjust for any cultural factors. In particular, Catholic countries show a high correlation of GDP per capita with the political stability index and a significant negative correlation between tax revenue and economic strength, see Fig. 2.6.

The higher values for Catholic countries can be explained indirectly by the higher variance in the value of the political stability index there. A linear regression of GDP per capita as a function of the political stability index yields an index improvement by the value 1 for this group of

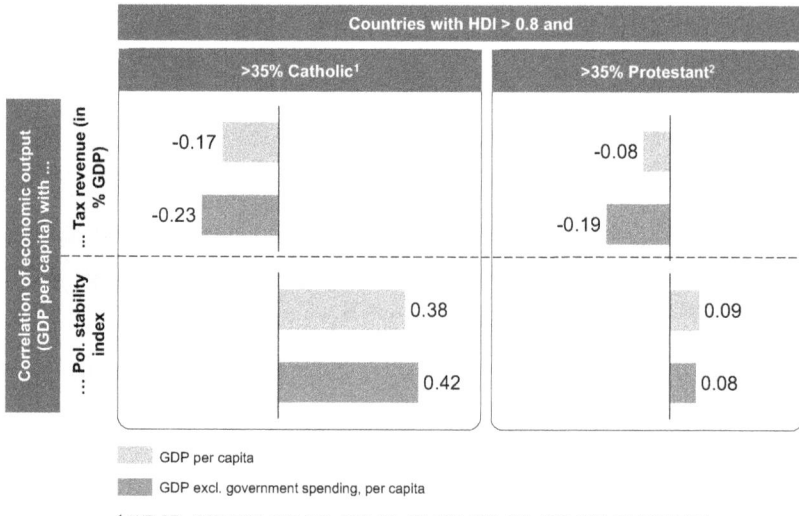

Fig. 2.6 Estimation of economic impact

countries, i.e., by 20% of the maximum interval by which the index is defined. This corresponds to an increase in GDP per capita of around $17,600 p.a. Clearly, the relationship between prosperity and political stability is not a one-way but a two-way relationship. Nevertheless, this value is considerable.

In the second step, we examine the drivers of political instability—inflation, government debt, and unemployment. Figure 2.7 shows the result of the rough analysis: While inflation and unemployment directly affect the constituents of the polity, the relationship is indirect for government debt. On the one hand, a high level of debt may indicate that the state has found it necessary in the past to "keep voters happy" by high spending. On the other hand, a high level of public debt may lead to erosion of confidence in the stability of the state, which may then become a self-fulfilling prophecy via elections and media behavior.

This rough analysis for industrialized countries with HDI > 0.8 thus also seems to indicate that domestic problems are major drivers of political instability.

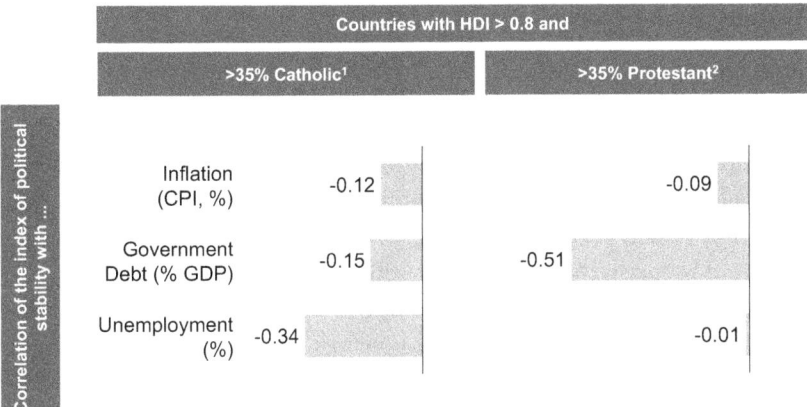

Fig. 2.7 Drivers of instability

In addition to these measurable criteria, "social psychology" can also play a role in assessing a state's domestic political stability. Strauss and Howe (2009) describe a cyclical movement of such a psychological basis, according to which a major crisis event such as a war, pandemic, or the like occurs at regular intervals.[5] The crisis period is characterized by drastic, rapid actions by the central authorities—in other words, a period of high political uncertainty.

In summary, it can be said that there is a significant increase in the probability of political risks occurring in jurisdictions when there is high pressure—whether of an economic or psychological nature. This is why it is important for the company to prepare for such phases at an early stage. Conversely, the probability of these risks typically decreases when a domestic or foreign political conflict has been conclusively resolved and when prosperity increases noticeably.

---

[5] The authors describe four stages of about 20 years each, with the fourth stage representing the crisis. This results in cycles of a total duration of approx. 80 years, the typical time span of a human life.

Foreign Policy Drivers

Just as the state can come under pressure from its domestic counterparties, this can also occur with regard to its foreign counterparties. Political escalations and economic wars are only two of many scenarios. Even a small relative decline of the local jurisdiction compared to its competitor can put it under pressure. This kind of pressure can have a destabilizing effect and increase the likelihood of political risks.

A simple indicator of a jurisdiction's view of a certain competitor is the way it deals with its ambassadors as well as its behavior in international bodies, such as the United Nations. Moreover, there is a connection between the domestic and foreign policy dimensions, for example, when a domestic crisis is to be contained by emphasizing an external threat.

Long-term Drivers

In addition to a jurisdiction's current situation, long-term factors also play a role. These include the long-term economic level at which the local society operates. A low level has a particularly destabilizing effect if it makes the state a pawn in the game of changing "elites," whether internal or external.

Even more important may be the social capital of the local society, namely the level of mutual trust. Ultimately, a lack of trust, on the one hand, and the desire for political change, on the other, can be regarded as the main fundamental or long-term drivers of political insecurity.

> **Conclusion: Summary**
>
> The main findings of this chapter are as follows:
>
> 1. We define political risks (in the narrower sense) as potential future actions by the jurisdiction with a negative impact on the company.
> 2. In general, political changes can also have a positive impact on corporate value; strategic management of political risks takes this into account.

3. There are four important classification options for political risks: the specificity of the risk, the value stream affected, the actor and financial value drivers. Classification by financial value drivers is particularly useful for assessing risks.
4. Political risks play such a major role in both economic and business terms that their specific treatment is justified.

References

Bekaert, G., & Harvey, C. R. (2000). Foreign speculators and emerging equity markets. *The Journal of Finance, 55*(2), 565–613.

Bekaert, G., Harvey, C. R., Lundblad, C. T., & Siegel, S. (2014). Political risk spreads. *Journal of International Business Studies, 45*(4), 471–493.

Bharathy, G. K., & Silverman, B. (2012). Applications of social systems modeling to political risk management. In *Handbook on decision making* (pp. 331–371). Springer.

Buchanan, J. M., & Tullock, G. (2003). What is public choice theory. *Rationalizing capitalist democracy: The cold war origins of rational choice liberalism, 133*.

Corsetti, G., Kuester, K., Meier, A., & Müller, G. J. (2013). Sovereign risk, fiscal policy, and macroeconomic stability. *The Economic Journal, 123*(566), F99–F132.

Gebel, T. (2018). *Free Private Cities: Making governments compete for you.* Aquila Urbis.

Giambona, E., Graham, J. R., & Harvey, C. R. (2017). The management of political risk. *Journal of International Business Studies, 48*(4), 523–533.

Harvey, C. R. (2004). *Country risk components, the cost of capital, and returns in emerging markets.* Available at SSRN 620710.

Lerner, A. B. *Unpredictability in international politics: Risk, uncertainty, and complexity.*

McKellar, R. (2017). *A short guide to political risk.* Routledge.

Moran, T., & West, G. T. (2005). *International political risk management: Looking to the future.* Washington, DC: World Bank. https://openknowledge.worldbank.org/handle/10986/7430 License: CC BY 3.0 IGO.

Pfetsch, F. R. (2003). *Theoretiker der Politik.* Wilhelm Fink Verlag GmbH & Co KG.

PRS Group. https://www.prsgroup.com/explore-our-products/icrg/

Rousseau, J. J. (2017). *Der Gesellschaftsvertrag: Prinzipien des politischen Rechtes*. e-artnow.

Schulze, S. (2009). *Risikomanagement im Bereich politischer Risiken*. GRIN Verlag. https://www.grin.com/document/147068

Shapiro, A. C. (1985). Currency risk and country risk in international banking. *The Journal of Finance, 40*(3), 881–891.

Sottilotta, C. E. (2016). *Rethinking political risk: Concepts, theories, challenges*. Routledge.

Stephens, M. (1999). *The changing role of export credit agencies*. International Monetary Fund.

Strauss, W., & Howe, N. (2009). *The fourth turning: What the cycles of history tell us about America's next rendezvous with destiny*. Crown.

The Global Economy. https://www.theglobaleconomy.com/

Weber, M. (1921). *Wirtschaft und Gesellschaft. Grundriss der verstehenden Soziologie*. 1. Halbband, Tübingen, S. 28

Weber, M. (1972). *Wirtschaft und Gesellschaft*.

Weber, M. (1992). *Politik als Beruf*. Reclam.

Weimer, D. L. (2000). Review of the nature, estimation, and management of political risk, by J. Monti-Belkaoui & A. Riahi-Belkaoui. *The Journal of Risk and Insurance, 67*(4), 668–670. https://doi.org/10.2307/253856

Wikipedia. https://en.wikipedia.org/wiki/Country_risk

Yi, Y., Luo, J., & Wübbenhorst, M. (2020). Research on political instability, uncertainty and risk during 1953–2019: A scientometric review. *Scientometrics, 123*(2), 1051–1076.

3

Methods of General Risk Management

In this chapter, we introduce the terms and methods of general risk management that we apply to political risks throughout the rest of this book. A comprehensive explanation or discourse about these methods would go beyond the scope of our work. The chapter serves as a review for readers with a solid basic knowledge of risk management. However, in combination with standard literature, to which we give references, even an untrained reader should be equipped with the necessary theoretical tools needed for the further explanations on managing political risks.

Risk management is well developed as a functional discipline, so we can draw on an extensive toolbox of methods. However, due to the specific nature of political risks, not all methods can be readily applied. We demonstrate this in the following.

Figure 3.1 shows the generic process of risk management. On the one hand, it illustrates the operational process which companies conduct on an annual basis. On the other hand, it can also be interpreted as a "risk life cycle" of an individual risk: from risk identification to risk mitigation and control. The following three sections are structured using this process, with the last three process steps being summarized in Sect. 3.3.

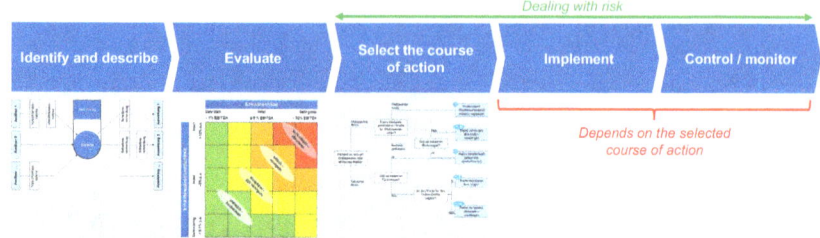

Fig. 3.1 Generic risk management process

3.1 Risk Identification and Description

Risks as unknowns with negative impact may be known to the company or not. A distinction must therefore be made regarding unknowns as to their level of inherent uncertainty and as to whether they have been identified by the actors at all. These two dimensions of unknowns were brought to public attention by Donald Rumsfeld's famous statement about "known unknowns" and "unknown unknowns" (Youtube, n.d.). Figure 3.2 shows our interpretation of this differentiation: One dimension shows whether the risk has been identified in the company; the other indicates whether there is a sufficient understanding of the risk and the corresponding uncertainty—ideally in the form of a thorough risk assessment.

Godfrey et al. (2020) assign different management methods to the four areas of this matrix (Godfrey et al., 2020):

- Known knowns are dealt with in *traditional risk management*,
- Unknown knowns, as possible events visible only to individual managers, are made transparent to the whole company and managed according to *enterprise risk management* (see Sect. 3.4),
- Known unknowns as well as unknown unknowns, i.e. known and unknown uncertainties that can also offer opportunities, are finally treated in *strategic risk management* (see Sect. 3.5).

In any case, the first risk management task is to reduce the area of the unconscious but relevant as far as possible, i.e., to *identify* and *systematize*

3 Methods of General Risk Management

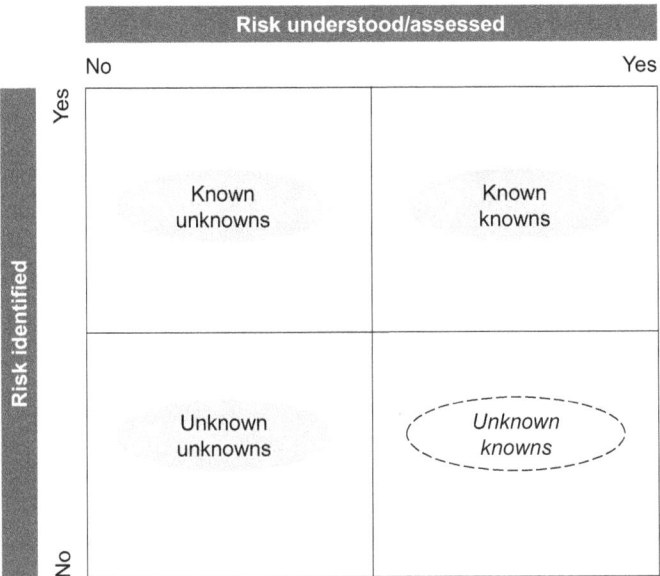

Fig. 3.2 Known-Unknown-Matrix

existing risks. The necessary methods are presented in Hopkin (2018). Different methods can be used to *identify risks*: recording existing knowledge in the organization (questionnaires, brainstorming), detailed examination of specific processes or systems (audits), and structured identification along the company's value drivers or processes (driver trees, flowcharts). The PEST framework is used to record external risks, such as political, environmental, social, and technological unknowns. The PEST framework in the form of detailed threats is included in the SWOT analysis during strategy development. Figure 3.3 shows the common risk identification methods. They are aimed at using both the expert knowledge available in the organization and external knowledge.

The subject of risk *systematization* or *categorization* is often handled in general risk management using the following three categories:

- Strategic risks are deliberately taken to gain a competitive advantage or because they are inherent in the business model.

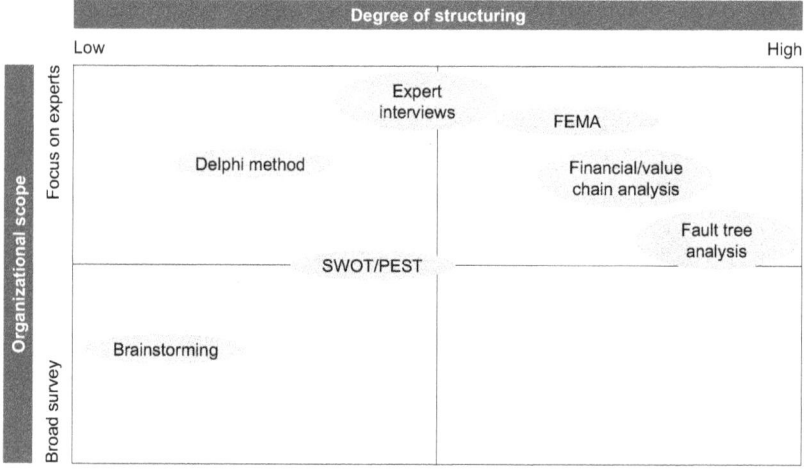

Fig. 3.3 Overview of risk identification methods

- Speculative risks are typically symmetrical in terms of positive and negative impact on the company. They are taken consciously, typically by trading on liquid markets and when investing.
- Other operating risks typically represent a necessary side effect of the business model. These include regulatory risks with a limited impact on businesses.

Instead of these three types, we simply distinguish between strategic and tactical political risks (see Sect. 4.4): This distinction is more relevant for the question how to deal with a specific risk.

The second step, after risk identification and categorization, is the risk *description*. A qualitative description helps create a common understanding and forms the basis for estimating the risk's impact and likelihood. This includes:

- Naming the sources or triggers of the possible event.
- Describing the event itself—what is happening in detail.
- Describing the risk impact and the measures that might reduce it. For this purpose, we can use the FIRM framework: finances, infrastructure, reputation, and market are the dimensions used to describe the impact.

3 Methods of General Risk Management

The "Bow-Tie" template shown in Fig. 3.4 summarizes the results of the risk description.

This template is particularly suitable for risks with a *discrete random variable*. The simplest case of such a risk has only two possible future states: (1) "event occurs" or (2) "event does not occur".

Cases with graded impact are somewhat more complex, e.g.

- "Event occurs with 100% of the maximum damage",
- "Event occurs with 30% of maximum damage", and
- "Event does not occur".

In practice, there is often a *continuous* random variable. This is the case, for example, with speculative risks, where the market price of a good or security can assume a continuous spectrum of values. If a company's success is exposed to the fluctuations of such a price, we represent the damage—or the benefit—by a probability distribution. In the case of political risks, for example, tax rates or price and quantity specifications come into play as quasi-continuous random variables. The company

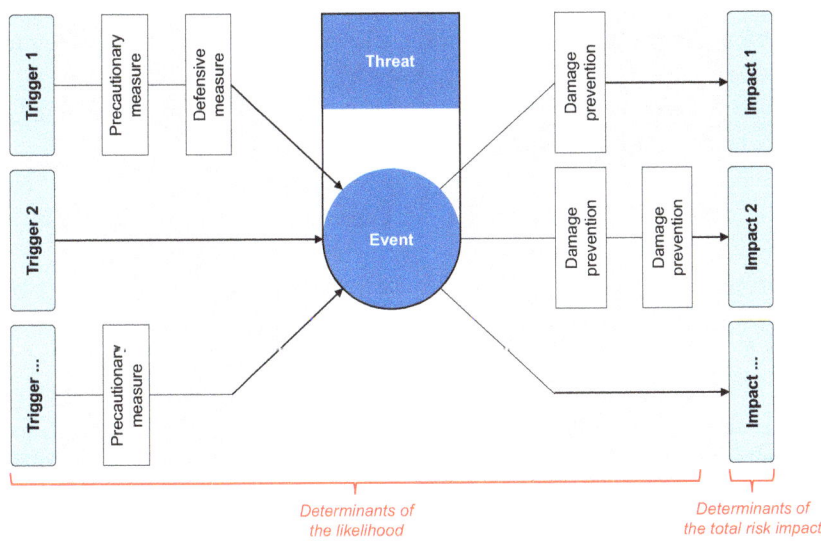

Fig. 3.4 Risk description based on "Bow-Tie"

needs to decide for each individual case how risks with graded impact or continuous random variables can be described best. In many cases, an extended "Bow-Tie" template, where the event is recorded in a more differentiated manner, serves this purpose.

Section 4.1 describes how to identify and describe political risks.

3.2 Risk Assessment

Classic risk assessment can be merely qualitative or also include quantitative analyses, depending on data availability. In the following, we briefly outline the general method. In Sect. 4.2 we discuss the topic in more detail, specifically for political risks.

For risks with discrete random variables, we can analyze the two core dimensions of *impact* and *likelihood* separately. These two dimensions can then be separated in the risk description, as shown in Fig. 3.4. The assessment also includes an estimate of the time dimension, i.e., when the harmful event may occur and the duration of possible damage.

A simple template for representing these two dimensions is the risk matrix, see Fig. 3.5. Here, the impact and the likelihood are assessed by coarse ranges or orders of magnitude. The risk matrix facilitates the comparison of several risks and thus helps with prioritization.

For risks with a continuous random variable, the quantitative analysis differs in the following two respects:

1. The impact is not described as an absolute value but as a function of the random variable.
2. The probability distribution of the random variable substitutes the likelihood of a discrete event.

In essence, this determines the probability distribution of the impact. For these kinds of risks, an extensive scientific field has been established, which deals with risk quantification and hedging (Damodaran, 2007; Markowitz, 1952; Trigeorgis, 1995; Sharpe, 1964; Lintner, 1965; Mossin, 1966). Key elements are the portfolio theory according to Markowitz as well as probabilistic methods like decision trees and Monte Carlo

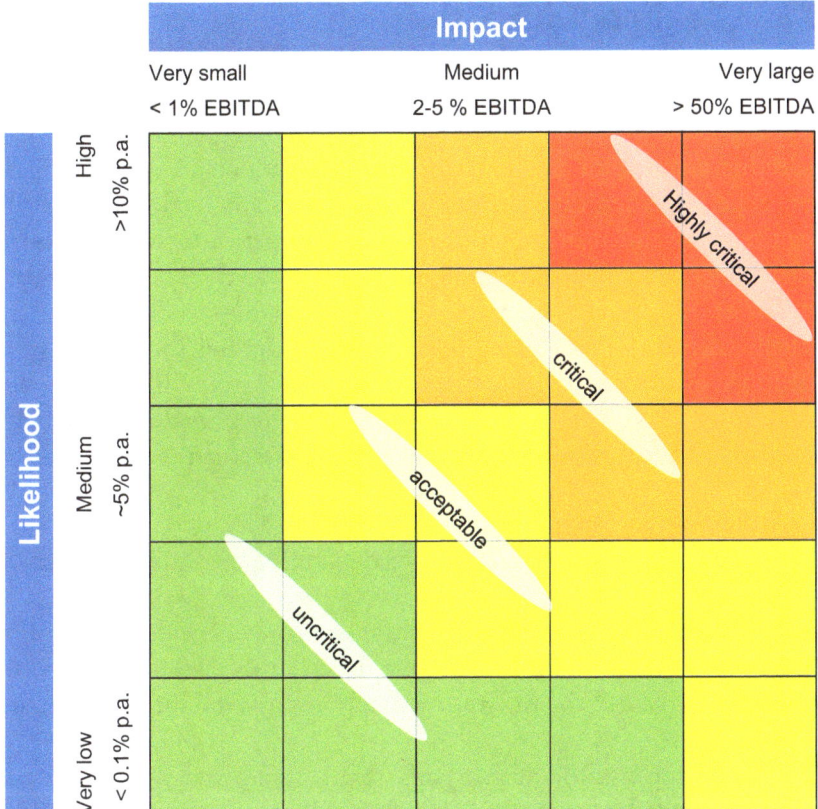

Fig. 3.5 Risk matrix: impact versus likelihood

simulations. Portfolio theory, for example, deals with the question of how to structure an optimal investment portfolio from a risk-return perspective. Since in this book we not only take the manager's perspective but also that of the owner, the view of the company as an investment is quite relevant. We will come back to this in Sect. 3.5. However, the above-mentioned methods require a high level of available data to determine the impact and probability distributions.

Finally, any quantification of risks should consider the fact that most unknowns can also represent opportunities for the company.

3.3 Dealing with Risks

3.3.1 Step 1: Selecting the Course of Action

Selecting a course of action starts with the question of the risk significance, i.e., whether it is a strategic or tactical risk. Strategic risks typically require involvement of ownership or top management; tactical risks can usually be managed at the middle-management level.

Tactical risks as an undesirable side effect of a business activity should usually be reduced or avoided in some form. Options for action can be identified along the two dimensions of the risk matrix: The goal can be a reduction of the impact and a reduction of the likelihood. The following four options are frequently mentioned in the literature:

1. Avoiding risk, namely, avoiding the risky activity.
2. Reducing risk, which includes a reduction of the impact and/or the likelihood.
3. Bearing or accepting risk; this option is mainly considered for minor risks, such as operational or project risks. In this case, it is usually sufficient to control the risk appropriately and to establish a budget and time buffer.
4. Transferring risk to another party that is in a better position to take the risk, e.g., by insurance or hedging; this corresponds to a reduction of the risk impact—the likelihood is not affected by this.

These four options are also known as the 4Ts of risk management (Hopkin, 2018):

– Terminate → Avoid risk
– Treat → Reduce risk (if necessary, also avert risk)
– Tolerate → Bear risk
– Transfer → Transfer risk

A mere reduction of the likelihood, i.e., averting the risk, is not explicitly mentioned in this listing but is an aspect of options 1–3. For the sake of completeness, we add this as a fifth option. Figure 3.6 assigns the resulting options to the risk matrix.

In the end, we obtain a list of options that is overcomplete: The first three options differ by the degree of risk reduction, and the last two options differ by the lever. As a rule, the company decides in the first step about the degree of risk reduction (options 1–3); the second step deals with the risk reduction levers (options 4 and 5). It is therefore justified to further consider all the five options even though they are partly redundant.

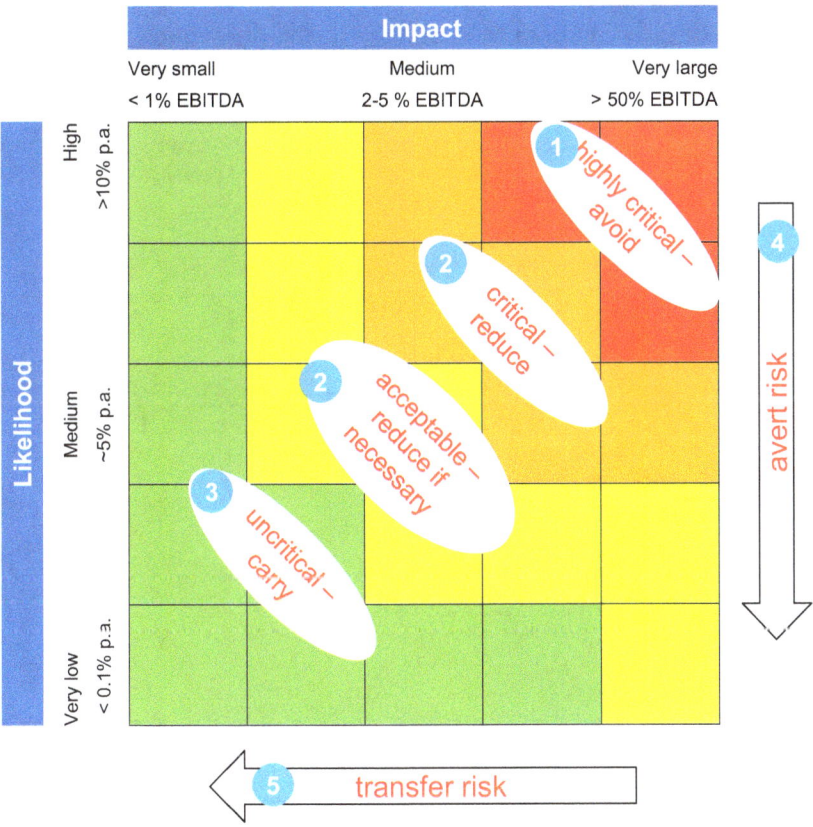

Fig. 3.6 Options regarding course of action for tactical risks

Strategic risks are distinguished from tactical risks. On the one hand, they include the risks threatening the existence of the company, which are classified in the top right of the risk matrix. They exceed the company's risk tolerance and should be avoided or transferred. On the other hand, they include risks that are deliberately taken because the company wants to gain a strategic competitive advantage related to the risk. The objective of these risks is then to maximize value creation. In the above structure, this is a special case of bearing the risk (option 3).

The options for action related to strategic and tactical risks can be summarized using a decision tree, as shown in Fig. 3.7.

Symmetric risks, whose expected value has no impact on the company, can also be included in this framework. Instead of the impact, one uses the costs directly incurred by dealing with the risk, which are primarily the opportunity costs of the tied-up risk capital. The options for action then basically correspond to actions for non-symmetric risks.

Specific aspects of dealing with political risks are discussed in Chaps. 5, 6, 7. It should be considered that these risks are caused by human

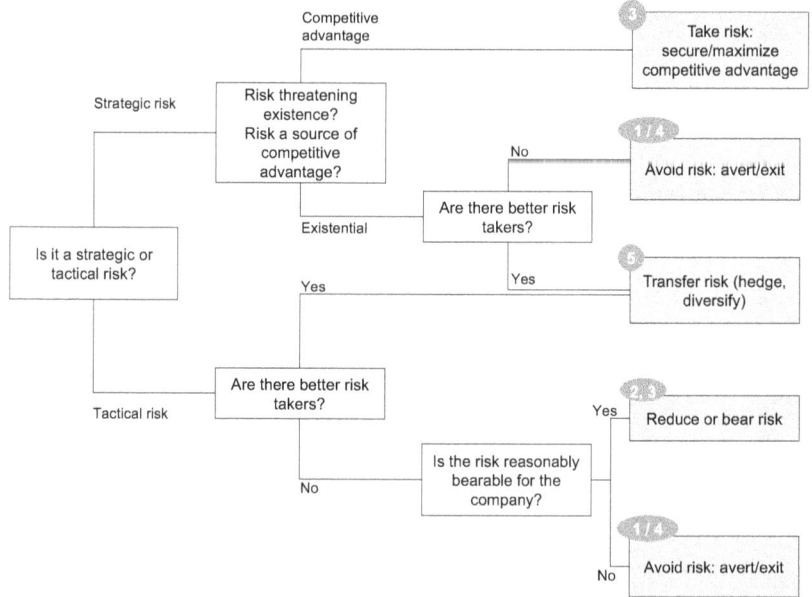

Fig. 3.7 Exemplary decision tree for dealing with risk

actors and typically affect many or all companies in a jurisdiction. Although this often prevents the option of insurance, it creates new opportunities for dealing with the risks.

3.3.2 Step 2: Implementation

Implementation differs significantly depending on which course of action has been selected. In principle, the specific tasks can affect all functions of the company and have an impact on products and services, methods, structural and process organization, and information technology. Accordingly, risks are often managed outside the risk management function. For example, hedging of symmetrical price risks is the responsibility of the company's internal procurement or trading department, transfer of risk is the responsibility of the "Insurance" function and meeting regulatory requirements is the responsibility of "Compliance". Specific measures are implemented in projects, or the line units concerned. However, risk management is responsible for identifying, processing, and monitoring risks. In Sects. 5.5 and 6.6, we address topics relevant to implementation of political risk management.

3.3.3 Step 3: Risk Control

Monitoring or control of risks can be understood as a sub-discipline of controlling. Quantitative risk controlling is based on indicators such as the "value at risk" which, e.g., measures the risk arising from a securities position. Risk limits can then be defined, or sensitivities calculated for such indicators, see, e.g., (Damodaran, 2007). Such quantitative methods are widely discussed in risk management literature.

These methods are only somewhat applicable to risks that are difficult to quantify. However, the basic idea of a risk limit can be transferred. Such a limit is set as a threshold value for a specific risk indicator over the longer term. If the limit is exceeded (limit breach), the decision-makers are informed by the responsible operating unit and involved in solving the problem. In addition, specific measures are defined ex ante that should be implemented upon limit breach, such as selling the securities carrying the risk. For risks that are difficult to quantify, this warning mechanism can be replaced by qualitatively defined events that indicate an increase of likelihood. These kinds of events are referred to as *trigger points*. When they occur, they trigger ex ante defined measures as well as information and decision processes. This form of risk control, also referred to as trigger point tracking, will be discussed in Sect. 4.3.

Finally, the company needs to monitor the implementation of concrete measures to deal with risks. If specific actions are implemented in a project, project controlling methods are applied. If measures are implemented in the line organization, the generic management instruments apply. Since these forms of control are not specific to risks, we will not detail them any further.

3.4 Embedding in Corporate Organizations

The procedures and organizational embedding of risk management have undergone a significant change in recent decades. In the 1970s, the focus was on controlling or avoiding specific individual risks. These risks were typically managed in the appropriate operating unit. The increasing importance of risk management then culminated in the concept of enterprise risk management (ERM). Enterprise risk management aims at comprehensive management of all risks relevant to the enterprise (Frahm, 2019). Finally, in this century, the strategic aspect is gaining importance, concerning the question of which risks are essential for the corporate strategy, both in negative and positive terms, see Fig. 3.8. In the following, we will provide an overview of the most important elements of enterprise risk management (ERM).

Key topics of enterprise risk management (ERM) are *risk portfolios, risk appetite, and risk-bearing capacity, organizational implementation,* and *integration* into corporate strategy, see Fig. 3.9:

- The term *risk portfolio* refers to a comprehensive view of all the critical risks as well as their internal and external drivers. This also includes analyzing the dependencies between the individual risks, e.g., in the

3 Methods of General Risk Management

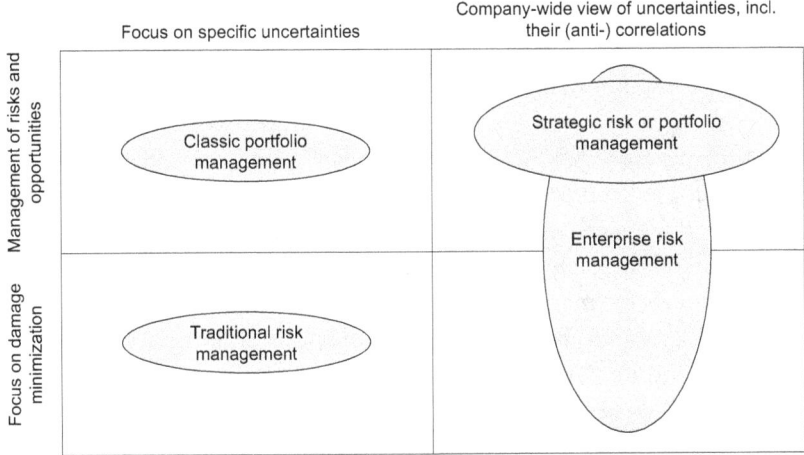

Fig. 3.8 Development stages of general risk management

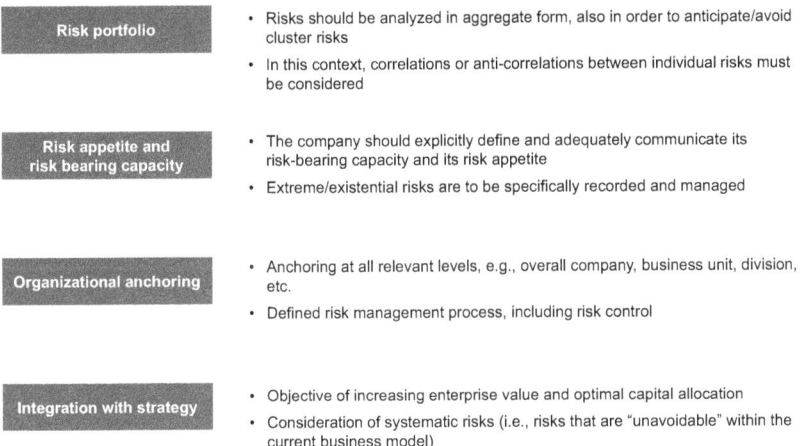

Fig. 3.9 Selected elements of enterprise risk management

form of correlations and anti-correlations. This contrasts with traditional risk management, which analyzes individual risks and how they are handled.
- The company's *risk appetite* and *risk-bearing capacity*, that is the willingness and financial capacity to take risks, must be clarified. This con-

trasts with an approach that is aimed exclusively at avoiding or reducing risk and considers the fact that taking risks can be an essential part of the business model or strategy. Based on this clarification, the company defines risk limits and suitable measures to prevent the limits from being exceeded.
- A further key feature of enterprise risk management is its comprehensive *organizational implementation*, as opposed to the management of individual risks solely in the area concerned. This also includes a structured process for managing all portfolio risks, embedding risk management in all key decisions of the company and linking it with internal auditing and internal communications.
- Finally, ERM explicitly considers the potentially strategic nature of risks and calls for *integration* of risk management into the corporate strategy. This includes clarification regarding the risks that the company consciously takes to achieve its goals as well as evaluating the management of these risks in relation to the strategic success factors.

Various standards have been developed to formalize the requirements for comprehensive risk management in line with ERM. Examples include ISO 31000 and the COSO ERM (Moeller, 2007). Hunziker (2018) points out the success factors for introducing these kinds of standards (Hunziker, 2018).

For political risks, we delve into the topic of organizational implementation in the following sections:

- Operational aspects for dealing with tactical political risks, Sect. 5.5,
- Integration of political risks into the strategic management process, Sect. 6.5, and
- Operational aspects for dealing with strategic political risks, Sect. 6.6.

3.5 Strategic Risk and Portfolio Management

Classical risk management focuses on reducing or avoiding possible future loss events. In recent decades, as already mentioned, another perspective on risks has gained in importance (Godfrey et al., 2020;

Goodfellow & Raynor, 2004): A competitive advantage in dealing with or carrying the risk can represent a strategic success factor for the company. For example, a riskier course of action may promise lower costs, higher returns, or greater growth than a less risky one. This assumption seems plausible, especially if there is a reasonably functioning market where the two options compete to some extent. A simple example of such an option is investing in a (politically) unstable but low-cost production location, as opposed to investing in a more stable but more expensive location. A company that is better able to deal with the risks at the low-cost location than its competitors is more likely to be able to fully capture the cost advantage. This perspective is denoted as *strategic risk management*, which we apply to the class of political risks in this book.

While strategic risk management looks for competitive advantages in the context of risk, *portfolio management* theory deals with the relationship between risk and return. For liquid assets such as securities, these relationships have been studied in detail, see, e.g. (Markowitz, 1952) or (Trigeorgis, 1995). Based on historical data for the security, the risk is derived from the variability of its market price, and the expected return is derived from its historical return. A specific investment in a liquid asset or in a portfolio of such assets can then be plotted in what is called the risk-return diagram. The best investment portfolios in terms of high returns at low risks constitute the efficient frontier, which is defined for the entire sector or industry. In contrast, options or portfolios that are of equivalent utility to the company lie on the company-specific risk-return indifference curve. The intersection of the "best" indifference curve with the efficient frontier determines the optimal investment portfolio or, in our extended understanding, the best course of action.

This Markowitz theory, named after its originator, can also be applied to the problem of strategic investments by an individual company. The portfolio of securities is replaced by a portfolio of investable or disposable assets and business units. These are modeled as cash flow functions, driven by several input variables. The company can determine historical risk[1] and historical return[2] from historical values for these variables.

---

[1] Calculated as fluctuation margins of specific input variables.
[2] Calculated as the historical mean value of specific input variables.

Future developments can be analyzed through scenarios. We refer to this extension of Markowitz theory as *strategic portfolio management*.

Figure 3.10 illustrates strategic portfolio management for a power generation company with different technological investment options.

Application of this theory clearly presumes that the risks under consideration can be quantified. In Sect. 6.3, we will go into more detail on strategic portfolio management in the context of political risks.

> **Conclusion: Summary**
>
> The main elements of this chapter are the following:
> - Risk management can be described as a five-stage process, see Fig. 3.1.
> - A wide range of methods are available for risk identification, see Fig. 3.3.
> - The Bow-Tie framework is suitable for an overarching description of a risk, Fig. 3.4.
> - The risk matrix differentiates between the impact and the likelihood and thus provides the starting point for risk assessment, Fig. 3.5.
> - Options for dealing with risks can be selected using a decision tree, as exemplified in Fig. 3.7.

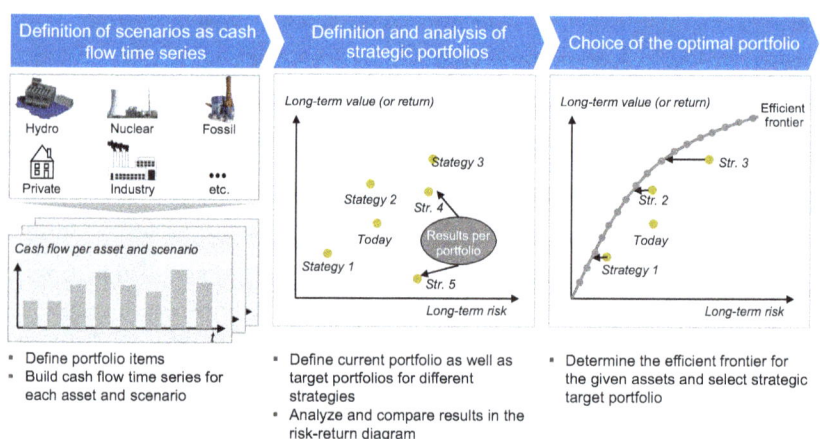

Fig. 3.10 Application of Markowitz theory to a power generation company

References

Damodaran, A. (2007). *Strategic risk taking: A framework for risk management*. Pearson Prentice Hall.

Frahm, G. (2019). *Enterprise Risk Management*, 1. Korr. Auflage, Herausgeber: MBA-Fernstudienprogramm, Koblenz.

Godfrey, P. C., Lauria, E., Bugalla, J., & Narvaez, K. (2020). *Strategic risk management: New tools for competitive advantage in an uncertain age*. Berrett-Koehler Publishers.

Goodfellow, J. L., & Raynor, M. E. (2004). Managing strategic risk: A new partnership between the board and management. *Strategy & Leadership*.

Hopkin, P. (2018). *Fundamentals of risk management: Understanding, evaluating and implementing effective risk management*. Kogan Page Publishers.

Hunziker, S. (2018). Erfolgskriterien von enterprise risk management in der praktischen Umsetzung. In *Ganzheitliches Chancen- und Risikomanagement* (pp. 1–28). Springer Gabler.

Lintner, J. (1965). The valuation of risk assets and the selection of risky investments in stock portfolios and capital budgets. *Review of Economics and Statistics, 47*, 13–37.

Markowitz, H. M. (1952). Portfolio selection. *Journal of Finance, 7*, 77–91.

Moeller, R. R. (2007). *COSO enterprise risk management: Understanding the new integrated ERM framework*. Wiley.

Mossin, J. (1966). Equilibrium in a capital asset market. *Econometrica, 34*, 768–783.

Sharpe, W. F. (1964). Capital asset prices: A theory of market equilibrium under conditions of risk. *Journal of Finance, 19*, 425–442.

Trigeorgis, L. (Hg.). (1995). *Real options in capital investment: Models, strategies, and applications*. Westport.

Youtube. https://www.youtube.com/watch?v=REWeBzGuzCc

4

Create Transparency About Political Risks

As outlined in the last chapter, the first risk management step is to systematically uncover the risks relevant to the company and assess their impact and likelihood. In the first two sections, Sects. 4.1 and 4.2, identification and assessment methods for political risks are discussed in more detail and illustrated with examples. Section 4.3 briefly discusses methods for ongoing risk control. The final Sect. 4.4 makes the distinction between tactical and strategic political risks, which is essential for the chapters that follow.

4.1 Identify and Describe Political Risks

Our aim is to identify political risks affecting the company as systematically and as comprehensively as possible. The focus is on identifying all legislative, executive, and judicial uncertainties that can have a significant positive or negative impact on the enterprise value. To achieve this objective, a starting point is the assessment of political risks as described in Sect. 2.3. It can be useful to work in a very detailed way by identifying risks in different dimensions. For example, the company starts identifying risks in the originator dimension (legislative, executive, jurisdictional) and complements the results with identifying risks along the financial value drivers.

For identifying *legislative* risks, existing regulatory requirements are a good starting point: "How could these requirements be expanded or alleviated?" In addition, we can identify potential regulation along the areas that are highly relevant for the company. This can be done using historical comparisons, comparisons with other jurisdictions, expert surveys, and company and environmental analyses. A particular focus is on possible long-term developments. Such a fundamental analysis can then be complemented with an investigation of the current political discussion points that might lead to new regulation.

We can also identify *executive* and *judicial* risks based on the current and historical situation. Again, a combination of systematic or historical analyses and expert opinions can create a good starting point for further consideration.

We then check the resulting set of individual risks for completeness by examining the financial value drivers. For each driver, we look for possible future events with relevant impact and likelihood. The company can use the brainstorming method to overcome any status quo bias, generating unusual ideas in a risk-free setting. Ideally, the company also considers risks that might affect the planned future activities. In addition, risks can be identified in the company's value chains as well as in contractual relationships with customers, suppliers, and other counterparties.

Finally, we *describe* the risks based on the criteria shown in Sect. 3.1, typically in the form of the Bow-Tie diagram. Risks with discrete variables are differentiated from those risks with continuous random variables. Figure 4.1 illustrates these three steps for identifying and describing risks.

In the following, we introduce three company examples that are used throughout the rest of the text. The first two examples represent unusually simple situations that illustrate individual aspects of the method. The third example, however, represents a situation with very different types of political risk and thus illustrates the complexity that companies typically face in practice.

4 Create Transparency About Political Risks

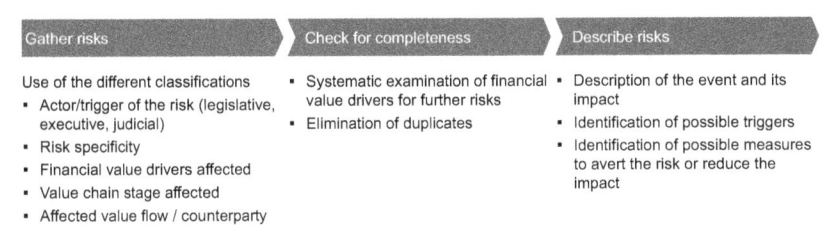

Fig. 4.1 Procedure for identifying and describing political risks

---

Example 1: Chemical Company

US chemical company in Pennsylvania in 2022: The cost of energy, in particular electricity, is a major share of the company's total costs. Pennsylvania's potential carbon-pricing policy would presumably lead to an increase of these costs. The company has identified the policy as a political risk and classified it as relevant for further investigation:

Introduction of carbon pricing → Risk of increase in electricity costs.[1]

Figure 4.2 shows the description of the risk by means of a "Bow-Tie" diagram.

Example 2: Independent Power Producer

European power generation company in 2014: This company has a broad mix of power generation facilities with different technologies—nuclear power plants, wind power plants, gas turbines, etc. Energy policy measures at the production sites can influence generation costs and sales prices as well as prohibit operation of certain generation technologies or impose additional, possibly prohibitive, costs. Figure 4.3 shows typical regulatory requirements in the European energy industry across generation, grid, trading, and sales.

Figure 4.4 shows an overview of the laws relevant for electricity producers in Germany and integration of these laws into EU law, as of 2014.

The company shifts the more precise specification of individual risks to the assessment phase, see Sect. 4.2.2. This example represents an extension of the "chemical company" example to a situation with several individual risks that are closely related.

---

[1] Typically, the chemical company would have to acquire CO_2 certificates itself. A lack of these certificates would increase costs. To keep the example simple, we assume that this is not the case.

> **Example 3: Commodity Trader**
>
> International commodity trader, based in Singapore, in 2022: The company trades metals, energy commodities, and agricultural products on a global scale. It owns storage facilities but does not operate any mines. It has identified the following relevant political risks:
>
> a. Financial market regulation: stricter requirements for financial transparency and capital endowment.
> b. Supply chain laws: application of a state's environmental protection requirements to all sites involved in the supply chain (mining, refining, transportation, etc.).
> c. Embargo against certain countries of origin, enforced through potential fines imposed on the company as well as sanctions against its decision-makers.
> d. Expropriation of storage facilities at certain sites.
>
> This example, with several unrelated or weakly related risks, thus comes closest to typical real-life challenges.

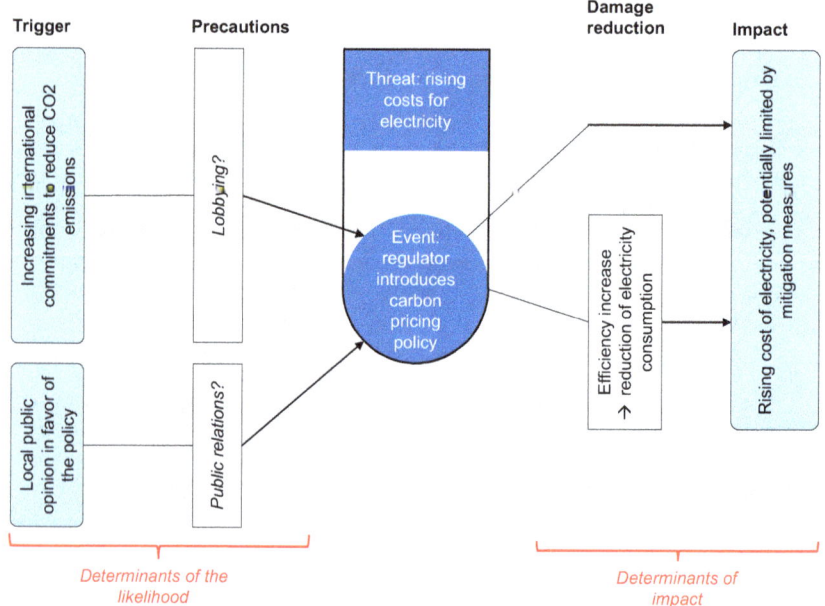

Fig. 4.2 Example (1) Qualitative risk description

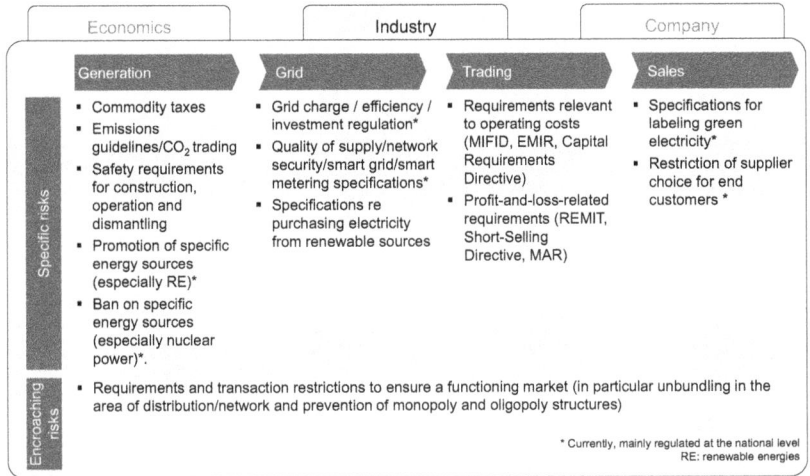

Fig. 4.3 Example (2) Regulatory requirements in the value chain of the European energy industry

4.2 Assess Political Risks

The next step is to determine how the risks we have identified and described affect the company.

> **Important**
>
> It is often difficult to quantify political risks. This applies above all to the risk likelihood: Political risks are man-made and are thus always subject to the unpredictability of free human will. The potential impact, however, can often be quantified with sufficient robustness.

Figure 4.5 shows three levels of risk assessment that differ in terms of accuracy. The first level A is typically used when a company's risks are assessed from the outside, e.g., by a bank analyst. It requires only superficial information but will hardly suffice to select a course of action.

Level B represents a simple form of risk assessment within the company. It is always used when the company lacks more detailed information about risks. We have already illustrated this method in connection

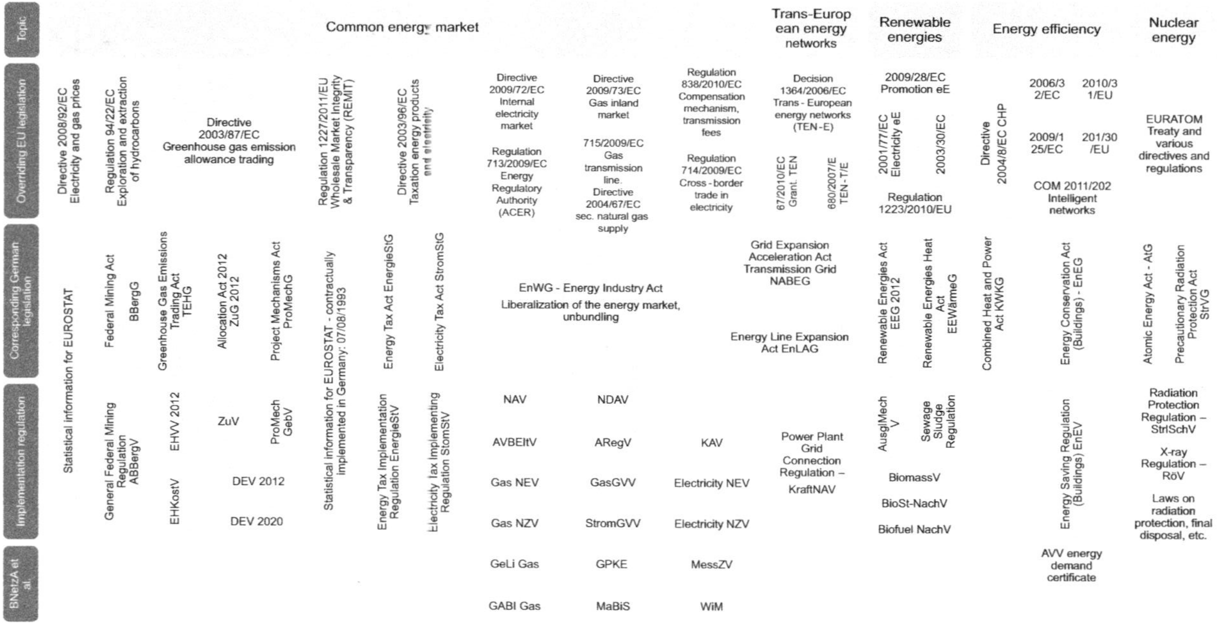

Fig. 4.4 Example (2) Overview of legal framework for the German energy industry

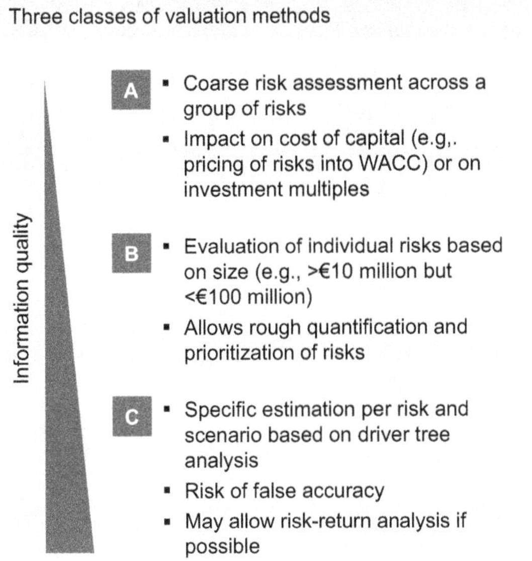

Three classes of valuation methods

Information quality (increasing)

A
- Coarse risk assessment across a group of risks
- Impact on cost of capital (e.g,. pricing of risks into WACC) or on investment multiples

B
- Evaluation of individual risks based on size (e.g., >€10 million but <€100 million)
- Allows rough quantification and prioritization of risks

C
- Specific estimation per risk and scenario based on driver tree analysis
- Risk of false accuracy
- May allow risk-return analysis if possible

Fig. 4.5 Overview of valuation methods

with the risk matrix, see Sect. 3.2. For the two dimensions of impact and likelihood, we build categories that differ by order of magnitude and allocate the risks into these. For the allocation, it is advisable to use several instruments such as

- historical and geographical analogies,
- expert workshops, or
- surveys,

if quantitative values cannot be used. The organizational skills required for estimation are ideally developed continually. Comparing the forecasted situation to the actual situation *ex post* provides important insights. Initially, such expert knowledge can often be obtained from external service providers.

In the following, we delve into Level C, which is the most accurate method. We first deal with assessing single risks. This case can be relevant when investigating individual operating units of the company that are exposed to only one material risk. The method is also applied in case of fully independent individual risks.

We then extend the method to the dominant case with several material risks that also exhibit interdependencies (or correlations, couplings). Our focus is on political risks, but the mathematical method is also applicable to other risk types and can be used across the board.

4.2.1 Evaluating a Single Risk

The quantification of an individual risk is divided into the two dimensions already introduced:

1. assessment of the impact, i.e., the potential damage when the isolated risk occurs, and
2. assessment of the likelihood.

The product of the impact and the likelihood yields the expected loss, which is also referred to as value at risk (VaR).

We first discuss risks with discrete random variables (see Sect. 3.2).

Quantifying the *impact* is straightforward in some cases. Political risks that have a clear impact on a specific financial driver, such as increasing the profit tax rate by a certain amount, are one such case. Another example is political risks with a clear impact on certain (pre)products for which there is a liquid market with transparent prices. The elasticities of the supply and demand sides can be obtained from the market data or from fundamental modeling. The influence of a specific political measure on the products' price and quantity—and thus the extent of the damage to the company—can be quantified comparatively well. In this case, the company can draw on an extensive body of valuation theory from general risk management, see, e.g., (Damodaran, 2007; Sharpe, 1964; Lintner, 1965).

It is possible, however, that the impact of political risk on the value of the company is more complex. In this case, it is useful to illustrate the relationship between the risk and its impact using a *driver tree model*. Classically, such a driver tree visualizes the impact of cost and revenue items on the cash flow of the company or business units by depicting the causal relationships between individual drivers (Klauck, 2015). From a financial perspective, the driver tree models the company or one of its business units.

Such a driver tree representation of the mathematical dependencies can also be used to evaluate the risk impact: The calculation of the financial indicators is formulated such that a specific uncertainty affects only one element at the lowest level of the tree. We call such an element the *risk driver*, as opposed to the (comparatively) stable drivers. The latter are sometimes referred to as *parameters*. A loss event corresponds to a change of the risk driver's value. This allows to analyze the effect of the risk on the financial key figures, such as cash flow.

The driver trees should be regularly compared with current regulatory trends and adjusted if necessary. They are also used when we assess multiple risks in Sect. 4.2.2.

The *likelihood* that a specific political risk will occur can only be roughly quantified: Political risks depend on complex political decision-making processes, and human free will, which cannot be analyzed precisely. Moreover, regulatory and other political interventions are often one-time events, and no historical empirical values can be used. However, the macroeconomic analysis of country risk may be useful in estimating the likelihood. Specifically, Belkaoui et al. (Predicting Political Risk, p. 135–139) suggest analyzing the following:

- Political actors: positioning, past behavior
- Fractionalization/polarization
- Stakeholder power map; war gaming
- Environment of the actors, e.g., legitimacy crises, upcoming elections
- Mass data analysis, e.g., of trending keywords connected with the risk

Such meta-analyses can eventually be summarized in the form of *scenarios* describing the future behavior of political actors. Ideally, we end up with a limited set of scenarios that comprehensibly and consistently describe the specific risk. These scenarios can be equally likely or have their own specific likelihood. In the simple case, a scenario merely corresponds to the occurrence of a specific risk. Then, its likelihood also corresponds to the likelihood of that risk. In any case, a high degree of business judgment is necessary to quantify the likelihood of the risk.

Scenario development is widely covered in the strategic management literature, see, e.g., (Damodaran, 2007; Miller & Waller, 2003). Figure 4.6 gives an overview of the most important steps for our purposes.

Political risks with *continuous random variables* are analyzed through a generalization of the method described above. In the example of the increase of the profit tax rate, we analyze the entire spectrum of possible values, e.g., from an increase of 0% up to 10%. The future profit tax rate assumes the role of a random variable.

In this case, the likelihood becomes a function of that random variable. Due to the difficulties described in determining likelihoods for political risks, it is usually not worth investing major resources in this task. At this point, the extensive method developed for financial market risks is not applicable to political risks. Rather, we again employ scenario analyses to capture possible future developments as comprehensibly and consistently as possible.

We now apply the method to our example of the chemical company.

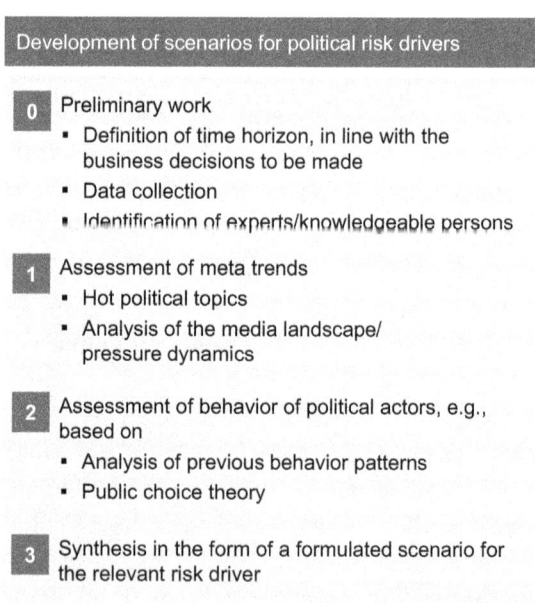

Fig. 4.6 Development of scenarios for political risk drivers

4 Create Transparency About Political Risks

Example 1: Chemical Company

As explained above, the company has only identified one relevant political risk, the carbon-pricing policy, resulting in an increase in electricity costs. The driver tree can be constructed in a simple way, see Fig. 4.7. The important point here is that the higher-level variables can be derived unambiguously from the lower-level drivers. In our example, earnings before taxes is a unique function of the drivers:

$$\text{EBT} = \text{Sales} - \begin{pmatrix} \text{costs of raw materials} + \text{price of electricity} * \\ \text{quantity} + \text{other costs of goods sold} \end{pmatrix}$$
$$- \text{other costs}$$

As shown, the price of electricity is the only risk driver, since only it would be affected by the carbon-pricing policy. The quantitative relationship between carbon pricing and the electricity price can be determined from historical data or from a microeconomic analysis. The company may also be able to obtain this analysis from a service provider.

This creates the essential prerequisites for quantifying the impact for a specific risk scenario. In our example, the company finds that the carbon policy would result in an electricity price increase of 20% over the next 3 years, compared to the current level.

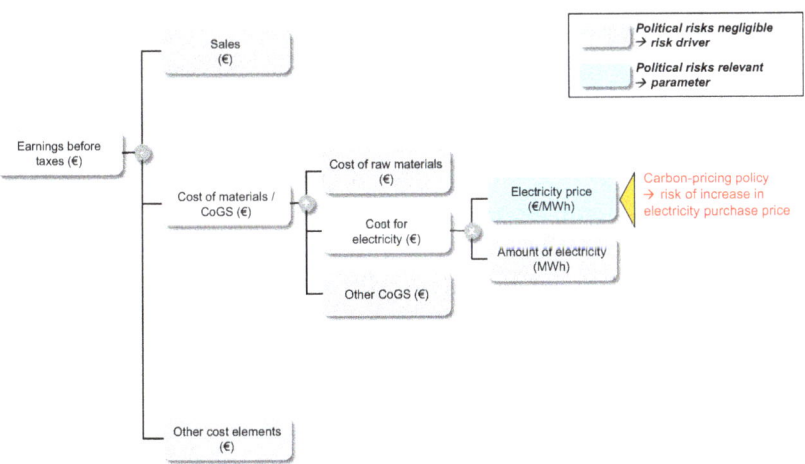

Fig. 4.7 Example (1) Driver tree

4.2.2 Evaluating Multiple Risks

If the company is exposed to more than one risk, it might not be sufficient to merely assess the impact and likelihood for each individual risk: The risks may be interdependent, in other words, correlated or coupled. We can analyze such coupled risks in two ways:

1. Determination of the "copula" between the individual risks and formation of the "copula-weighted sum"; in the simplest case, the copula is the correlation of two discrete events.
2. Scenario-based aggregation, e.g., in the form of a Monte Carlo simulation.

In connection with regulatory requirements, the Bank for International Settlements explains these two methods in a user-friendly manner (BIS, n.d.).

The first method assumes that all the relevant risks can be quantified with some accuracy, including the copula between the risks. However, this approach is difficult for an entire company. For one thing, the company will have a hard time estimating copulas. This situation worsens with continuous risk variables. Attempts to map such a complex risk structure in a mathematically exact way will either produce pseudo-accuracy or fail completely.

Because of this, the second method is generally preferable for aggregating political risks. The formation of scenarios was discussed in Sect. 4.2.1 above. Many companies already employ this method, for example in stress testing. Therein, typically, the company analyzes the impact of a worst-case scenario for a specific type of risk (univariate scenario analysis).

Multivariate scenario analyses, on the other hand, are common practice when forecasting securities or commodities prices at trading houses. This approach maps risks and correlations between risks based on several scenarios, which can be analyzed and evaluated individually. One scenario describes a set of possible outcomes of strongly correlated risk variables. The use of this method for aggregating political risks is described in the following.

4 Create Transparency About Political Risks

The complete procedure appears complex at first glance but has stood the practice test. It can be divided into five steps (see Fig. 4.8), of which we have already covered the first two (Figge & Otto, 2013):

Step 1

Identification and *description* of risks, see Sect. 4.1.

Step 2

Linking risks with financial indicators: development of *driver trees*, see Sect. 4.2.1.

Step 3

Qualitative assessment of the coupling (correlations) between individual risks: *derivation of risk clusters*.

We group the individual risks such that risks in the same cluster show significant coupling among each other. Risks in different clusters, on the other hand, have negligible coupling. The need to precisely determine correlations is thus eliminated. In principle, however, quantified correlations can also be processed mathematically, e.g., by analyzing the respective correlation coefficients (r_{ij}) between two individual risks i and j. In this case, the likelihoods of the scenarios we discuss in the next step depend on the respective r_{ij}.

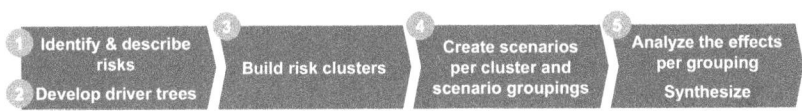

Fig. 4.8 Procedure for evaluation in the case of multiple risks

Step 4

Formation of *scenarios per risk cluster*: For each risk cluster, we formulate a reasonable number of scenarios, including their quantitative impact on the risk drivers in the cluster. Thereby, we describe future developments in the considered period for all the risk drivers in the cluster. In addition, we determine or estimate the likelihoods for each scenario.

As mentioned above, one can draw on a variety of tools for this step, such as historical and geographical analogies as well as expert workshops and opinion surveys. It is important to note that these tools are usually not created ad hoc but evolve continuously upon iteration of the risk management process. It is also important that scenarios be formulated along the time dimension, specifying trigger points or ramifications of a development path. We can then anticipate the business decisions to be made along this path.

For legislative risks, we can use the legislative process, including the roles of the executive and judiciary, considering the persons involved (e.g., in the form of a "power map over time").

Formation of *groupings of scenarios ("world")*: Once we have developed the scenarios for *each risk cluster*, we can combine them into *groupings of scenarios*, or "scenario worlds", e.g., scenario A1 (1st scenario for risk cluster A) combined with scenario B4 (4th scenario for risk cluster B) results in scenario grouping "A1–B4". The groupings contain assumptions on several uncorrelated risks, possibly from different driver trees, and thus represent an assessment for all company-related developments. If the likelihoods per scenario were also quantified in the previous step, the combined likelihoods per grouping can be determined from this as a simple product.[2]

---

[2] In theory, this assumes that the risk clusters are completely uncorrelated, i.e., decoupled. In practice, even with small correlations, the error of neglecting these is typically smaller than the unknowns of the estimation. In such cases, neglecting small correlations is justified since it does not reduce the quality of the analytic result.

4 Create Transparency About Political Risks

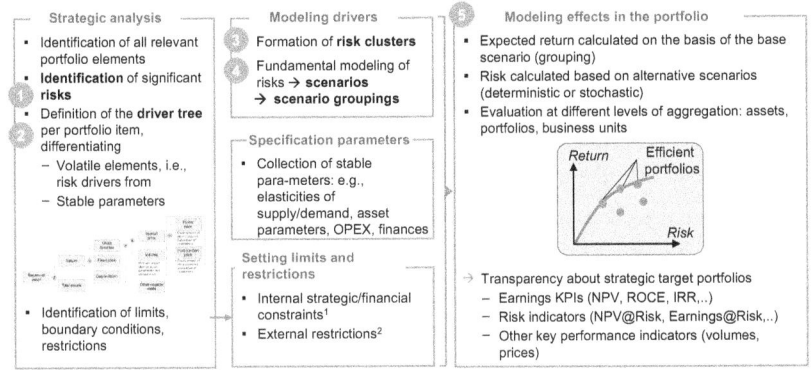

Strategic analysis	Modeling drivers	Modeling effects in the portfolio

• Identification of all relevant portfolio elements
• **Identification** of significant **risks**
• Definition of the **driver tree** per portfolio item, differentiating
  – Volatile elements, i.e., risk drivers from
  – Stable parameters
	Formation of **risk clusters**
	Fundamental modeling of risks → **scenarios**
	→ **scenario groupings**
		• Expected return calculated on the basis of the base scenario (grouping)
		• Risk calculated based on alternative scenarios (deterministic or stochastic)
		• Evaluation at different levels of aggregation: assets, portfolios, business units

	Specification parameters • Collection of stable para-meters: e.g., elasticities of supply/demand, asset parameters, OPEX, finances	

• Identification of limits, boundary conditions, restrictions	*Setting limits and restrictions*
	• Internal strategic/financial constraints[1]
	• External restrictions[2]
		→ Transparency about strategic target portfolios
		  – Earnings KPIs (NPV, ROCE, IRR,...)
		  – Risk indicators (NPV@Risk, Earnings@Risk,...)
		  – Other key performance indicators (volumes, prices)

[1] Strategic goals: markets, technologies, growth rates, etc. // Financial constraints: cash flow limits, risk-bearing capacity, etc.
[2] Regulatory constraints, public acceptance, etc.

Fig. 4.9 More detailed representation of the evaluation procedure

Step 5

Modeling of the *impact* on the portfolio or company.

Finally, we determine the impact for each scenario grouping using the driver trees. In other words, for each grouping, we calculate the key figures critical for corporate management, typically on the basis of annual cash flow (discounted cash flow method). As a result, we obtain one or more key figures for each grouping. This also completes the core of the assessment and can be used further, e.g., for selecting the optimal course of action.

With sufficient data points, we can perform a more detailed analysis in terms of expected value and variance by a Monte Carlo simulation; here, in turn, we can incorporate the weighting of the groupings based on likelihoods. If the data basis is not sufficient for a Monte Carlo simulation, the result is simply a set of groupings with associated key figures that provide the management with the action-relevant information.

It is important that the final preparation of the analysis result in a clear and understandable synthesis for the decision-makers.

This procedure can be supported by a tool as described in the Appendix B. Figure 4.9 shows an overview of the process supported by the tool. Using such an integrated tool offers clear advantages in terms of consistency and clarity compared with an analysis distributed among several tools.

We now return to our company examples.

> **Example 2: Independent Power Producer**
>
> The driver tree analysis yields five relevant risk drivers for the conventional power plants, as shown in Fig. 4.10. On the one hand, there are three drivers related to market prices (electricity, primary energy, CO_2 certificates) and, on the other hand, two technology-specific drivers (bans/phase-outs of certain technologies and increasing regulated risk commissions). For power plants with renewable electricity generation technology, there are three additional risk drivers that relate to the level of subsidies and the regulation of the priority regarding feed-in to the power grid, see Fig. 4.11.
>
> These eight drivers are interrelated by the topic of "energy policy" and are at least partially positively or negatively correlated. Accordingly, the company formulates comprehensive scenarios or scenario groupings that describe the characteristics for all drivers:
>
> – Scenario (A) "Continuation of energy transition": In this scenario, the risk drivers for renewable technologies do not materialize, subsidy levels and feed-in priority for renewables persist, which also means that the risk for conventional technologies does not materialize. The supply of CO_2 certificates will be reduced by 30% within 15 years, and a decision will be made to phase out all fossil generation technologies within 30 years. The remaining two risks (sanctions/risk commissions) do not materialize.
> – Scenario (B) "New focus on national self-sufficiency": Sanctions, tariffs, and other measures cause primary energy prices for hard coal, natural gas, and oil to increase by 100% uniformly within 10 years. The other risks do not materialize.
> – Scenario (C) "New focus on economic efficiency": Subsidies for renewables are reduced evenly over 20 years, and feed-in priority is eliminated in 10 years. The other risks do not materialize.
> – Scenario (D) "Status quo": In this scenario, the political and regulatory conditions do not change. It serves as the reference case against which the effects of the other scenarios are evaluated.
>
> Using these scenarios, the power producer can now quantify the impact for its power plant portfolio. Depending on the portfolio, the resulting impact may well be positive so that the company benefits from the policy

changes compared to the reference scenario (D). To continue the example, let us assume that the quantification of the impact yields the following results:

- Scenario (A) poses a significant threat to the company due to the phase-out of fossil generation technologies, reducing its asset value ceteris paribus by 80% within 30 years compared with scenario (D). At the same time, it also offers significant opportunities, as will be discussed in Chap. 6.
- Scenario (B), on the other hand, results in only a 15% reduction in asset value within 10 years, ceteris paribus, versus (D).
- In scenario (C), the asset value improves by 10% within 20 years compared to (D).

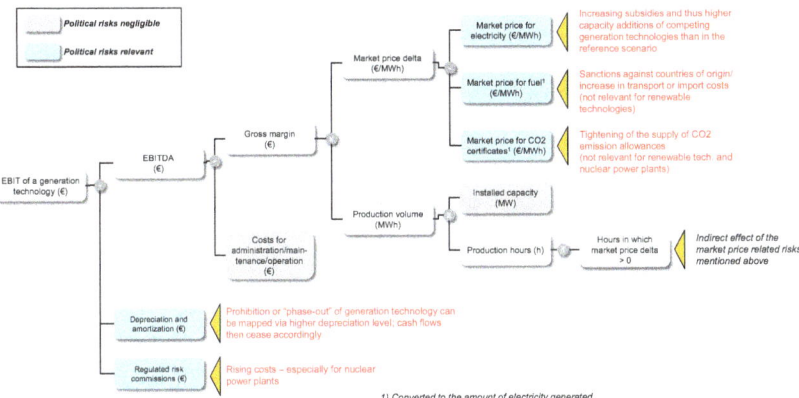

Fig. 4.10 Example (2) Driver tree for conventional power plants

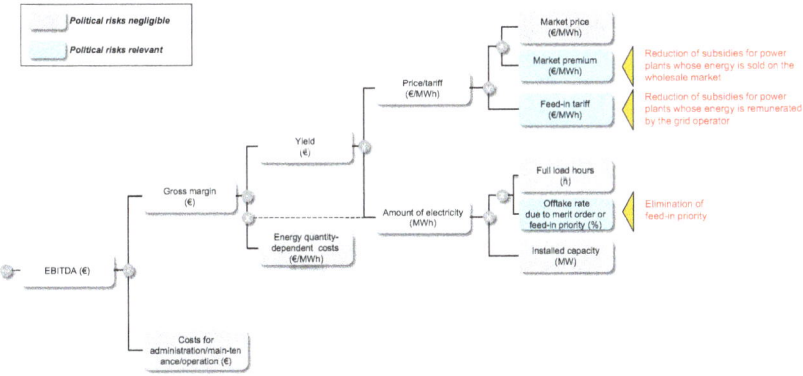

Fig. 4.11 Example (2) Driver tree for renewable technologies

Example 3: Commodity Trader

A driver tree that can be used to map the above-mentioned political risks can be found in Fig. 4.12. At the top level, we distinguish between an asset-intensive storage business and a mere trading business to separate the fourth risk (expropriation of storage facilities). The regulatory risks "tightening of financial market regulation" and "supply chain laws" influence the operating costs of trading, which we break down by functions. "Supply chain laws" and "embargo/sanctions" finally affect the revenue potential for specific commodities as well as geographies (countries).

The question is to what extent these risks correlate. On the one hand, tighter financial market regulation and supply chain laws both amount to interventionist policy. On the other hand, they have different political motivations: In the first case, the focus is on stability, with ethical and ideological considerations as a second concern. In the case of supply chain laws, on the other hand, ethical and ideological aspects dominate; stability hardly plays a role here. Finally, risks (c) and (d) are largely uncorrelated with (a) and (b). In turn, there is a weak correlation between (c) and (d) via the issue of geopolitical stability: Sanctions against those countries that enforce a policy of expropriation would be conceivable.

For the sake of simplicity—and to distinguish this example from the previous one—we assume in the following that the correlation of the individual risks is negligible. Then, for each of the risks, we design separate scenarios with at least two scenarios: the reference scenario and one scenario to describe the risk materialization. In our example, the reference scenarios simply continue the status quo. This does not have to be the case in practice but it simplifies the analysis. Moreover, we stick to one scenario per risk. We can then refer to the scenario where risk (a) materializes as "scenario A" and analogously for the other risks:

- Scenario A = Risk (a) materializes: Here, a law against market abuse is introduced within 5 years, which increases transparency requirements but does not entail any change in the business model or trading strategies for our commodity trader. The additional costs for compliance are calculated as 0.5% of company-wide EBITDA.
- Scenario B: The jurisdiction of the company's headquarters and its core trading unit enforces compliance with domestic environmental protection requirements for all of the company's sites and also for its direct suppliers (tier one) within 5 years. The associated costs are substantial, possibly threatening the business model. It is not possible to quantify these costs in any meaningful way, as they depend heavily on the specific form of the law, which is not yet available.
- Scenario C: In the risk case, another major commodity supplier, e.g., the Russian Federation, and the largest industrial state, e.g., the People's Republic of China, are cut off from trade with the other countries where

the company operates. This process takes two years. In the first instance, this eliminates gross margins (or Profit-and-Loss, PnL) in these countries. In the second instance, price volatility increases in the remaining markets, resulting in a 10% increase in affected PnL.
- Scenario D: The company's storage facilities are expropriated without compensation in two major jurisdictions within the next ten years. The quantification of the impact results in a reduction of the fixed assets by 30%.

Following this presentation of the assessment method for political risks, we now turn to the topic of ongoing risk and implementation monitoring.

4.3 Controlling and Monitoring

In the established risk management process, controlling follows the decision on how to deal with the risk. We will discuss this topic already here, as the method of controlling is closely linked to the risk assessment.

First, we distinguish between risks based on how easily they can be quantified. Risks that are easy to quantify (see Sect. 4.2.1) are regularly

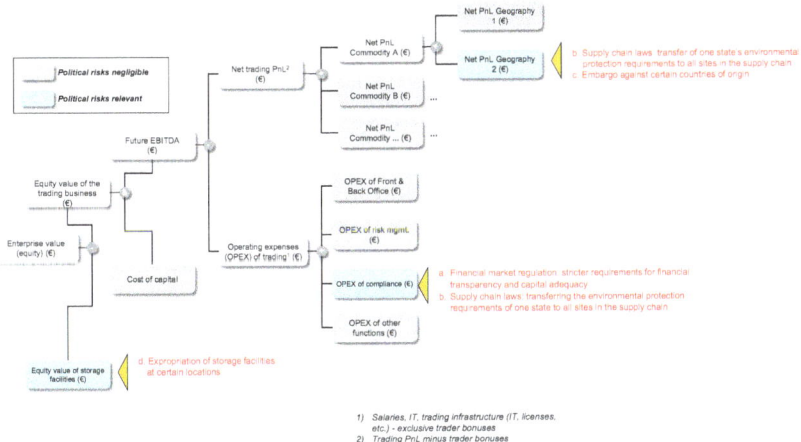

Fig. 4.12 Example (4) Driver tree for commodity trader

reassessed using the respective method, for example by evaluating the available market prices as an underlying for COGS. An extensive discipline of risk management and control has been established for trading highly fungible assets such as securities, commodities, etc., including the following steps (Hopkin, 2018):

(a) Definition of risk-bearing capacity and risk appetite.
(b) Definition of control elements, e.g., groupings of individual assets or deals into one book; definition of the corresponding control indicators, such as value at risk.
(c) Definition of limits for each book and indicator, as well as the measures to be taken upon limit breach.
(d) Regular calculation of the indicators and, upon limit breach, implementation of the defined measures.

The controlling and monitoring of risks that are difficult to quantify cannot be standardized. Depending on the risk, specific action is required. Even for such risks, it generally makes sense to define in advance the possible measures to be taken when the risk occurs or when a threshold value related to the risk is exceeded. This saves valuable time in the event of a crisis and aligns the company's organization with the same goal. Instead of a financial key figure, other observable events are used. In particular, the trigger points introduced above can be used for this purpose.

Ultimately, political risks are man-made: the occurrence of the risk is at the end of a human chain of action. That is why it is important to compare the anticipation of the risk with the actual situation at regular intervals to draw conclusions about risk likelihood and impact. The clearer the ex ante description of the risk, the easier it will be to carry out the subsequent monitoring process. Moreover, the regular comparison of anticipation and reality can train the company organization to improve the competence of anticipation. Ideally, over time, the organization's knowledge of the drivers, trigger points, and temporal developments of the risks grows continuously, independent of individual knowledge workers.

Once a trigger point materializes, or another critical development is monitored, this corresponds to the above-mentioned limit breach, triggering the execution of pre-defined measures. An example of such a measure is the withdrawal from a jurisdiction in the event of an illegal change of government (coup).

> **Example 1: Chemical Company**
>
> The risk of the new carbon-pricing policy is a classic political risk in the form of legislative changes or new regulations, which largely depends on political decision-makers. To continuously monitor the development of the likelihood and the impact, the company defines critical decision points, the trigger points, which are primarily based on the legislative process of specific jurisdictions.
>
> Figure 4.13 shows an overview of the Pennsylvania legislative process. In the simplest form, four levels can be defined:
>
> 1. *Discussion of* a legislative proposal (bill). This has usually already occurred, as the company would otherwise hardly have recognized the risk as critical.
> 2. *Introduction of the bill.*
> 3. *Adoption of the law.*
> 4. *Challenge* in court.
>
> In case of uncertain political majorities, it may make sense to further subdivide phases 2 and 3. The focus is on the scenario where the electricity price increases by 20% over the next 3 years compared to the current level.
>
> In addition, an analysis of the political majorities gives an indication of the likelihood of the change in the law. It can be based on public or proprietary opinion polls or on expert estimation.
>
> For documentation purposes, the new likelihood of the risk and the measures to be taken can be assigned to the decision points, see Fig. 4.14. For example, once the legislators have drafted the bill, the likelihood of the risk increases to 50%.

> **Example 2: Independent Power Producer**
>
> All the eight individual risks presented above are related to specific changes in laws or regulations and can be tracked via the trigger point method, and reassessed if necessary, in the same way as in example 1.

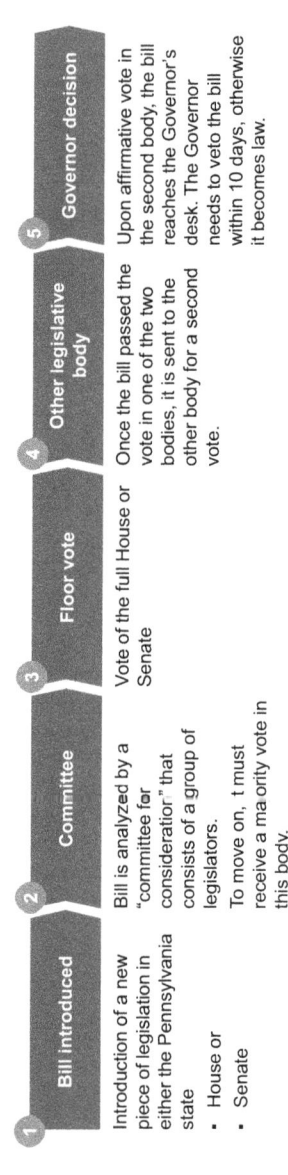

Fig. 4.13 Overview of the Pennsylvania legislative process

> **Example 3: Commodity Trader**
> Here, we distinguish between the risks of (a) financial market regulation and (b) supply chain laws, on the one hand. These kinds of risks represent "ordinary" changes in legislation and are to be monitored as in the first two examples. The risks of (c) sanctions or embargoes and (d) expropriation of storage facilities, on the other hand, result not only from regular domestic development but also disrupt foreign policy as contain revolutionary components: Sanctions are typically a reaction to a changed foreign policy situation. Expropriations, on the other hand, profit from an element of surprise (otherwise they might fail) and often trigger a reaction by other jurisdictions. Trigger point monitoring must take these dimensions into account. For an initial assessment of the foreign policy dimension, periodicals in the field are useful, e.g., Foreign Affairs magazine for the USA, even if they hardly provide quantifiable information. For the domestic disruptive dimension, political volatility drivers such as price inflation for basic goods are relevant.

In practice, controlling and monitoring of political risks will differ significantly according to their strategic importance. In the following section, we take a closer look at this dimension.

4.4 Distinction Between Tactical and Strategic Risks

The distinction between political risks of a tactical and strategic nature is essential for dealing with them. In general, *tactical risks* influence or impact the implementation of the corporate strategy. The strategy or business model of the company itself, however, is not affected. Management of these risks focuses on avoiding or reducing them. For political risks, we can follow the classic methods of risk management.

Strategic risks, on the other hand, are an integral part of the corporate strategy. On the one hand, they may endanger the existence of the company. On the other hand, they can have a significant impact on the competitive position, both positively and negatively. Generally speaking, the strategic importance of political risks is increasing.

We therefore differentiate political risks based on two criteria: the risk impact and its strategic importance.

4.4.1 Differentiation Based on Impact

Strategic risks have a significant impact on the corporate strategy due to the potential damage they may cause. They exceed the company's risk *tolerance*, i.e., the level of risk the company is willing to take. Tactical risks jeopardize the achievement of the objectives derived from the strategy. They exceed neither the company's risk-bearing capacity nor its risk tolerance.

4.4.2 Differentiation Based on Strategic Importance

Political risks that do not exceed the company's risk tolerance can, nonetheless, take on strategic significance. This is the case if the company expects a strategic advantage from taking the risk, i.e., if the potential upside outweighs the downside. Such an upside can exist independently of the company's competitors; we then speak of an *absolute upside*. In the opposite case, the upside exists only relative to the competitors—a *relative upside*. In both cases, strategic risk management focuses on identifying or developing *competitive advantages* related to risk.

At the top level, two sources for competitive advantages come to mind:

1. The company has a competitive advantage in *dealing* with risk, e.g., distinctive skills for managing and reducing risk. Examples include financial and commodity traders with regard to market price risk.
2. The company has a competitive advantage in *taking* the risk, e.g., a strong balance sheet. This is the core business of insurance companies.

Companies can exhibit a competitive advantage also for symmetrical risks, where the immediate opportunities and risks for the company

4 Create Transparency About Political Risks

balance each other out. This is typically the case if the company has special skills in operational risk management.

In ambiguous cases, the delineation between strategic and tactical risk is a business decision.

To illustrate the distinction between tactical and strategic risks, we return to ou three examples.

> **Example 1: Chemical Company**
>
> The individual risk described above, a 20% electricity price increase, represents a tactical risk for the company, as it does not have a significant impact on the corporate strategy, and the company does not gain a competitive advantage from bearing the risk. A significantly larger price increase, on the other hand, could become a serious threat to the company and would then constitute a strategic risk. The company can therefore define a threshold value, e.g., an increase of ≥50%, above which the risk becomes strategic.

> **Example 2: Independent Power Producer**
>
> In Sect. 4.2.2, we presented the scenarios that the company uses to assess the correlated individual risks:
>
> - (A) "Continuation of energy turnaround" → Reduction of asset value by 80% within 30 years; but also significant opportunity
> - (B) "New focus on national self-sufficiency" → Asset value reduction by 15% within 10 years
> - (C) "New focus on profitability" → Increase in asset value by 10% within 20 years.
>
> (A) is strategic; (B) and (C) are tactical. However, the groupings are completely anti-correlated since the occurrence of one scenario grouping means precisely that the other two will not occur. The company therefore treats the entire risk cluster as one strategic political risk.

> **Example 3: Commodity Trader**
>
> Here, the situation, in a nutshell, is as follows:
>
> - Scenario A → Increase in compliance costs by 0.5% of EBITDA → Tactical risk (a)
> - Scenario B → The associated costs are substantial for the company, possibly also threatening its existence → Strategic risk (b)
> - Scenario C → Loss of gross margins (PnL) in affected countries and increase of PnL in residual markets for the affected commodities by 10% → Tactical risk (c)
> - Scenario D → Reduction of the company's fixed assets by 30% → Strategic risk (d).

Important

According to the distinction, we further elaborate the examples or scenarios in different chapters, namely:
- Tactical risks: Examples (1), (3a) and (3c) → Chap. 5;
- Strategic risks: Examples (2), (3b) and (3d) → Chaps. 6 and 7.

Conclusion: Summary

The most important elements of this chapter may be briefly summarized:
- Political risks are typically identified based on the criteria described in Sect. 2.3. Once again, the Bow-Tie framework helps describe the risks, Fig. 3.4.
- Assessing these risks, in particular quantifying the likelihood, is often difficult. In this case, it is suitable to present the risk impact using driver trees. This formulates the key financial indicators in such a way that the drivers which are subject to significant uncertainty can be written as isolated variables, see, for example, Figs. 4.7, 4.10, or 4.12. Scenarios then allow us to quantify both the impact and the likelihood.
- To evaluate multiple risks, it is advisable to form risk clusters, whose impact, in turn, is examined by scenario analyses, see Fig. 4.9.
- Controlling/monitoring is typically carried out using the trigger points identified in the risk description, see, e.g., Fig. 4.14.
- Strategic risks are distinguished from tactical risks either by their magnitude and/or their strategic importance for the company.

Decision point	Likelihood new	Optional: impact new	Measure
a) Legislators draft bill	50%	unchanged	To be defined below (e.g., initiate discussions with government representatives to co-author the proposed legislation → lobbying)
b) Legislative Reference Bureau checks bill/committee vote	95%	unchanged	To be defined later
c) Voting in the two chambers (House and Senate)	80%	unchanged	To be defined later
d) Governor votes → implementation	100%	unchanged	To be defined later
e) Contest in state court → block	50%	unchanged	To be defined later
f) Supreme court decision	50%	unchanged	To be defined later

Fig. 4.14 Example (1) Description of the decision points for the "carbon-pricing policy" risk

References

BIS. https://www.bis.org/publ/joint25.pdf.

Damodaran, A. (2007). *Strategic risk taking: A framework for risk management*. Pearson Prentice Hall.

Figge, L., & Otto, M.-F. (2013). Regulatorische Unsicherheiten als Herausforderung für das Risikomanagement. *Energie – Markt – Wirtschaft, Heft, 1*, 13.

Hopkin, P. (2018). *Fundamentals of risk management: Understanding, evaluating and implementing effective risk management*. Kogan Page Publishers.

Klauck, S. (2015). *Enterprise simulations based on value driver trees*. Proceedings of the 8th Ph. D. retreat of the HPI research school on service-oriented systems engineering, 8, 111.

Lintner, J. (1965). The valuation of risk assets and the selection of risky investments in stock portfolios and capital budgets. *Review of Economics and Statistics, 47*, 13–37.

Miller, K. D., & Waller, H. G. (2003). Scenarios, real options and integrated risk management. *Long Range Planning, 36*(1), 93–107.

Sharpe, W. F. (1964). Capital asset prices: A theory of market equilibrium under conditions of risk. *Journal of Finance, 19*, 425–442.

5

Managing Tactical Political Risks

The starting point of this chapter is the nature of tactical political risks: They arise because of the company's strategy, but do not change it. The company should consider how to reduce (a) the negative impact and/or (b) the likelihood of these risks. The two approaches differ in theory but can complement each other in practice. In Sect. 3.3, a decision tree for handling general risks was presented, showing the company's options *before the loss event occurs*. We apply this perspective in Sect. 5.1 to political risks.

We then address the question of how the company can respond to the potential damage *after the event has occurred* (Sect. 5.2). In doing so, we consider the fact that human institutions cause political risks. Thus, dealing with a political risk that has occurred can be viewed as an interaction between two parties: the jurisdiction and the company. This perspective builds on the discussion in Sect. 2.2 and Appendix A. The combination of both perspectives, *ex ante* and *ex post*, results in a more differentiated and complete view of the potential courses of action in Sect. 5.3.

Finally, we address how these options are selected in practice (Sect. 5.4) and which factors must be considered during implementation (Sect. 5.5).

5.1 Ex Ante Options for Action

In the classical approach, which refers to the phase before the risk materializes (ex-ante), there are basically five options for dealing with tactical risks, see Sect. 3.3, Fig. 3.6:

1. Avoid risk,
2. Reduce risk,
3. Take risk, (the first three options being distinguished according to *urgency*), as well as
4. Avert risk, and
5. Transfer risk

that describe *how* risks are reduced at the top level. In the following, we want to specify this generic menu of options by a practical decision tree for political risks.

In practice, the first question is whether the political risk for the company can be *transferred* or *averted*. Option 4, risk aversion, refers to the case in which the likelihood of the risk is effectively reduced or eliminated for all affected economic entities in the jurisdiction. Risk transfer, option 5, on the other hand, focuses on reducing the potential impact specifically for the company. If possible, risk transfer is usually easier to implement than complete risk aversion. Therefore, we first deal with the question of whether the risk can be meaningfully transferred.

A *risk transfer* adds value if a better risk taker can be found. Such a better risk taker is characterized by the fact that he expects a lower (relative) impact from the risk than our company. This may be due to internal pooling or portfolio effects—as is the case with insurance companies—or due to better abilities for dealing with risk, e.g., an information advantage regarding the likelihood of the risk. In other words, the better risk taker has a skill advantage regarding the risk. The following sub-options exist for a risk transfer:

(a) Often, the risk can be partially or fully *insured*; the better risk taker is then the insurance company, which can use pooling effects as well as a strong capital structure. Insurance against political risk is particularly available for investments in developing countries. Examples include the US International Development Finance Corporation (DFC) as an agency of the US government or the Multilateral Investment Guarantee Agency (MIGA), a unit of the World Bank Group. Another example is the International Credit Insurance & Security Association (ICISA), an association of insurers that insures US exporters against counterparty default. This coverage is available regardless of whether political or private sector actors cause the default (DFC, n.d.).

Insurance of political risks in industrialized countries, on the other hand, is atypical.

(b) Secondly, the company can also *sell* the risky activities. The better risk taker is then the buyer who takes over the risky activities. This option is usually relevant to strategy and requires an appropriately high level of management attention.

(c) Finally, *diversification* of risk can also be subsumed under the rubric of risk transfer. For diversification, the company makes investments—or pursues analogous activities—which internally compensate for the risk exposure. In hedging, this is done by using financial market products. Strictly speaking, the company improves its ability to bear the risk, i.e., becomes a better risk bearer itself.

Examples: A wholesaler who fears that import duties will be imposed procures additional, domestic, suppliers that would not be affected. An electricity producer who fears falling electricity market price due to technology subsidies invests in these technologies.

If the company cannot find a better risk taker, the second step is to ask whether the risk can be *averted*. In practice, it is important to lobby the relevant political decision-makers. We illustrate this kind of lobbying in the following section. In most situations, the company can hardly rely exclusively on lobbying, if only because sooner or later other political decision-makers will appear whose motivations cannot be assessed today. Hence, an exclusive focus on averting represents a special case.

In the third step, the question arises as to the *acceptability or bearability* of the risk. The absolute upper limit is derived from the financial strength of the company, its risk-bearing capacity, as well as its risk tolerance. For obvious reasons, the risk tolerance is typically lower than the risk-bearing capacity. We therefore refer to this, going forward. If the risk does not exceed this tolerance level, we examine the profitability of the alternatives. In the simplest case, we compare the value of the risk-bearing business activities—neglecting the risk—with the expected negative value of the risk. If the expected value of the risk exceeds the value of the activities, it is clearly not advisable to bear the risk. Even if the risk expectation value is slightly below the value of the business activities, exiting can be the preferred option. Specifically, it is then advisable to terminate those activities since no buyer was found in the first step.

However, if the company is able and willing to bear the risk, it can still investigate as a final step whether the level of risk can be *reduced* by appropriate measures. All the above-mentioned options come into play again—but now as gradual measures such as partial insurance or partial reduction of the business activities at risk. This also includes lobbying with the more realistic goal of reducing the likelihood or the impact. In summary, we obtain the decision tree shown in Fig. 5.1.

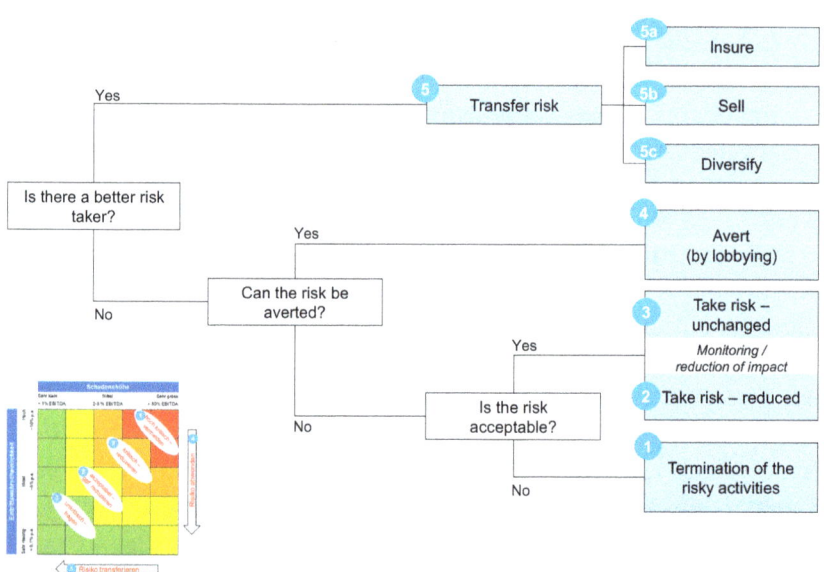

Fig. 5.1 Decision tree for ex ante handling of tactical political risks

Whenever the company bears a risk, whether in full or reduced, it should take measures for comprehensive risk management. On the one hand, this includes monitoring, i.e., regularly checking developments associated with the risk. For example, potential regulatory changes need to be identified at an early stage. On the other hand, a defined process is necessary if the situation deteriorates, e.g., in the form of taking further measures to reduce the risk.

In the following, we will now consider the situation where the risk has already materialized.

5.2 Ex Post Options for Action

To examine the options for action after the risk has materialized, we consider the fact that political risks are invariably caused by people: While natural risks mostly represent exogenous, unchangeable conditions, the cause of political risks, the political actors, can be regarded as *counterparties of the company*. New or amended laws relevant to the company as well as unexpected, direct damage by the executive or judiciary then represent possible actions of the counterparty.

Due to the state's monopoly on the use of force, which generally exists in industrialized countries, its actors will only act unilaterally in exceptional cases or extreme situations, e.g., by freezing bank accounts. In the vast majority of cases, they will pursue their goals by amended laws or regulations, with penalties for noncompliance. This shifts the implementation costs to the company, which is more efficient for the jurisdiction. In these cases, political risk materializes as a threat to make the company accept the changed legal situation.[1] This raises the question of how to *respond* to the threat.

In a model situation with only two parties, the initiator and its addressee, the possible responses to a threat can be described using the option tree in Fig. 5.2. In our case, the initiator is the jurisdiction, and the addressee is the company. In the first step, the question is whether the

---
[1] In Appendix A, we classify such threats as an essential component of *cratic actions*.

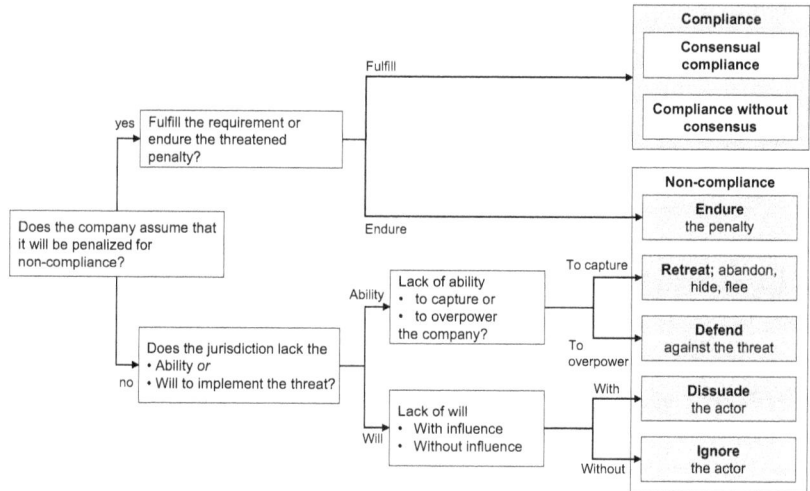

Fig. 5.2 Option tree for reaction to threat

company takes the threat of the jurisdiction seriously, i.e., whether it actually expects to be punished in case of noncompliance. If this is the case, it can only decide between complying or enduring the punishment (upper branch of the decision tree). Otherwise, we need to examine why the company does not take the threat seriously. Namely, why it believes that the jurisdiction will not successfully enforce the threat (lower branch).

This produces six main options, shown in Fig. 5.2 as blue boxes:

- *Compliance* or meeting the jurisdiction's requirement; this can be done with or without the consensus of the company.
- *Enduring* the consequences of non-fulfillment, i.e., passivity by the company.
- *Withdrawal of* the company, e.g., by moving out of the jurisdiction.
- *Defense* against the jurisdiction, e.g., physically preventing enforcement of a law.
- *Dissuading* the jurisdiction from its requirement, e.g., in the form of lobbying with the aim of reversing the policy measure after the fact.
- *Ignorance* of jurisdiction.

The option of defense typically does not apply if the jurisdiction's monopoly on the use of force is intact. The ignorance option only makes sense in those special cases where the jurisdiction is too lazy to enforce a rule that its leaders have bothered to put into law. Even enduring the threatened consequence in the absence of cooperation will seldom be the company's optimal response since the political actor will set the penalty higher than the cost of compliance. So, in many cases, only the following three options remain relevant:

1. Compliance
2. Dissuasion
3. Withdrawal

In an extended interaction model, the company can involve a third party. If the third party is not inferior to the jurisdiction in terms of strength, the options of defense or ignorance come back into consideration. An example is a US-based company whose investment in a developing country enjoys protection—implicit or explicit—by its guarantor, the government of its home country. Finally, the company can also transfer the risk consequences to a third party by an insurance policy. As explained above, this decision is made based on who is the best risk taker.

In the following, we illustrate the three ex post options for action that are most relevant in industrialized countries and evaluate them from a normative and practical perspective.

5.2.1 Compliance

This option is the standard for political risks with low impact. Ensuring compliance, also known as compliance management, enjoys a high level of attention in business management literature. Standards have even been established, such as ISO 37301:2021 (ISO, n.d.). The abbreviation CMS stands for Compliance Management System, which is subdivided into the following topics:

- Goals of compliance management: this includes comparing the company's values and the regulatory requirements; in the sense of classic compliance management, the company's values can only justify additional measures that exceed the regulatory requirements.
- Compliance Management Program.

  - Analysis of the regulatory requirements as well as the risks associated with compliance.
  - Guidelines to ensure compliance across the business functions.
  - Monitoring compliance with these guidelines.
  - Organizational and cultural aspects.
  - Communication and information, both internal and external.
  - IT Systems Support (Soft Guide, n.d.).

- Governance, i.e., responsibilities, reporting lines, and measures if guidelines are violated.

The success factors in compliance management largely correspond to those in risk management. On the one hand, the program needs to be designed to suit the company. This includes considering the current practice, the size of the organization, and the company's history. It is essential that the corporate values can be clearly translated into the compliance management guidelines. Secondly, it is important to ensure that the company's management shows sufficient commitment, that the right tools are used to detect violations, that the measures taken for violations are defined and adhered to in a targeted way, and that employees are adequately trained in this area. Further information on this topic can be found in (Singh & Bussen, 2015) or (Schulz, 2020).

From the political risk management perspective, a tightening of compliance requirements by the jurisdiction represents political risk materialization. Examples are increased requirements for transparency, increases in taxes and duties, or raising standards regarding the environment, employees, suppliers, etc., which are summarized under the acronyms SHE (Safety, Health, Environment) or ESG (Environment, Social, Governance).

From a normative point of view, the question arises as to whether the new requirement is justified. From the company's perspective, this amounts to the question of whether the requirement aligns with the company's values. If yes, one could argue that the company has previously acted in contradiction to its values (not fulfilling the new requirement). In that case, the contradiction is eliminated or reduced through compliance. However, this is quite unlikely.

Alternatively, one could argue that the company's values continuously adapt to the current legislation, requiring continuous implementation of new regulatory requirements, i.e., compliance. This overlaps with the case where the company has no values of its own but continuously and unreflectively adopts the values propagated by political actors. Only in these cases would universal, uncompromising compliance be the option of choice.

In the absence of these cases, the normative aspect speaks against full-fledged compliance. After all, the company is supporting the behavior of an institution that can unilaterally change the rules of the game due to a power imbalance. Of course, compliance can make sense for pragmatic reasons, in keeping with the motto "Pick your fights wisely".

5.2.2 Dissuasion/Lobbying

We have already mentioned lobbying as a key example of dissuasion. We understand the term broadly, for example, including donations to political parties and candidates. The success of this approach, which can be visualized, for example, by the performance of the Strategas stock market index, has already been discussed in Chap. 1. In the literature, the different varieties, target groups, and success factors of lobbying are treated broadly. A distinction is made at the following levels:

- Direct vs. grassroots lobbying: This distinction concerns the primary target group. In the first case, the lobbyist directly addresses the political decision-makers, in the second case, his or her (potential) constituency.

- Transactional approach vs. relationship-based approach: Influencing the policymaker by direct lobbying can take the form of a "trade" if the lobbyist in some way helps the policymaker achieve his or her goals. This would include direct bribery, most of which is punishable by law. The relationship-based approach, on the other hand, aims to influence the decision-maker at an emotional or ethical level.
- Individual vs. collective lobbying: The distinction is based on whether the company pursues its goals on its own or joins forces with fellow stakeholders.
- Differentiation by tactics: This is about which means are used in a specific situation or relationship, e.g., delivery of information, personal favors or help with winning over voters.

Success factors cited include the following:

- Early recognition of opportunities and risks of lobbying, as well as anticipation of future political decision-makers and positioning as well as influenceability.
- Bargaining power.
- Personal contacts and relationships.
- Specific solutions that can be realistically implemented by the decision-maker.
- Grassroots mobilization, as a primary or secondary approach.
- Continuous monitoring of the project along the political process.
- Flexibility regarding (less important) adjustments to specific projects.
- Ability to maintain an overview while mastering the relevant (legal) details.
- Good judgment, in terms of timing, people, and the feasibility of specific projects.

Gelak (2008) provides an industry-wide overview of this course of action to deal with tactical political risk (Gelak, 2008).

According to our definition, political risks only occur when political actors *change the previously existing "state of society,"* e.g., by changing a law, a regulation, or a judicial practice. Thus, a company that dissuades actors from making such a change usually reduces political risk for other companies or individuals as well. Clearly, others may be deprived of an opportunity if the status quo continues. It may also be that the company reduces the risk only for itself, e.g., by negotiating an explicit contract with the jurisdiction. This requires a certain balance of power between the company and the jurisdiction—accordingly, this sub-option tends to be used primarily in developing countries (Weimer, 2000).

However, lobbying can also be used for the opposite goal: to bring about a specific political action. This generally increases political risks for other companies and individuals. In practice, a large proportion of activities pursue this goal. We refer to this as *proactive lobbying*, as opposed to *reactive lobbying*, which seeks to preserve the status quo and reduce risks.

Our "dissuade" action option therefore only corresponds to reactive lobbying.

From a normative perspective, the latter, proactive lobbying, is problematic. It increases political risk and easily transitions into corruption and bribery. A clear case of bribery occurs when a company or an institution such as a trade association or NGO promises legislators a benefit in return for enacting a certain law. The law would usually be at the expense of third parties, e.g., taxpayers or consumers, whose choices would be restricted by product bans, import duties, etc. This would result in a loss of economic prosperity.[2]

An alternative to such explicit proactive lobbying is implicit proactive lobbying. It aims to endear oneself to certain actors, e.g., by political-cultural adaptation or various not-for-profit activities. Such indirect measures are legal and play an important role, e.g., in reducing investment risks in developing countries. From a normative perspective, however, they should not be undertaken by the company either, leaving only reactive lobbying as an ethical course of action.

5.2.3 Withdrawal

The standard case of withdrawal means moving away from the current jurisdiction. In contrast to lobbying and compliance management,

---

[2] In Germany, the more obvious forms of influencing the legislature have therefore been punishable under §108e of the German Criminal Code since 1994.

companies hardly use this approach systematically to deal with political risks today. Our contribution to closing this gap can be found in Chap. 7. A special case consists of making the company "invisible" and preventing access for the cratic actor. However, this is hardly a real possibility for companies in industrialized countries, is generally illegal, and will not be discussed further here.

5.3 Synthesis of the Options for Action

We now connect the options for action before the occurrence of the loss event (or risk materialization) with those after the occurrence. Figure 5.3 shows the resulting option space: If the company has already transferred the risk *ex ante*, averted it, or terminated the affected activities, the question of how to react to its materialization becomes irrelevant: The company then no longer suffers the risk impact. If, on the other hand, the company *bears the* risk—either in full or to a reduced extent—the entire

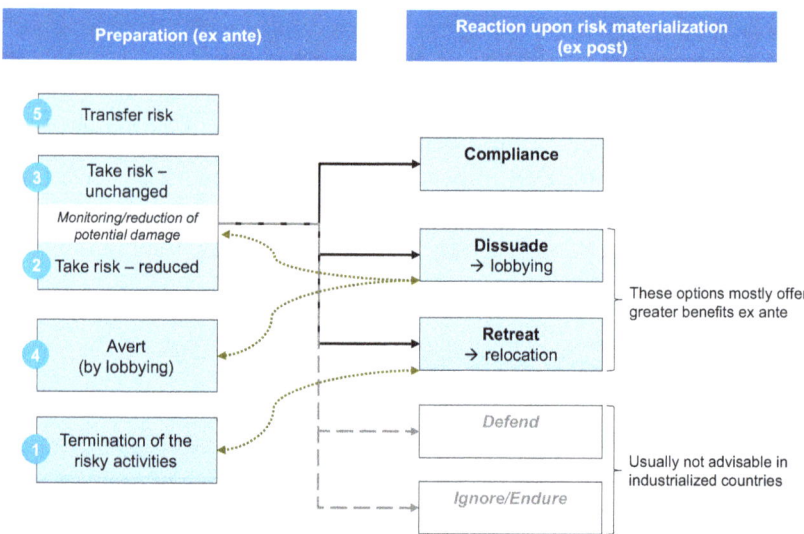

Fig. 5.3 Summary of the options for action

ex post option space can be considered in principle. In practice, three options stand out:

1. Compliance, i.e., adapting to the changed conditions.
2. Dissuasion of political decision-makers.
3. Withdrawal or departure from the affected jurisdiction.

For risks with limited effects, the company will typically comply with the new requirements. This explains the dominance in the existing literature on regulatory compliance. For risks with a significant effect, on the other hand, the options *dissuasion* and *withdrawal* should be considered. These have a much greater benefit if they are already taken, or at least prepared, ex ante: On the one hand, the probability of success is usually lower ex post than ex ante; on the other hand, the implementation costs are typically higher under high time pressure. The dashed curved arrows in Fig. 5.3 indicate this.

So, at the same time, *dissuasion* and *withdrawal* also represent opportunities for successfully *averting* the risk before it occurs. Focusing exclusively on dissuasion (lobbying) is usually not the best course of action. While some reduction in the risk may be achieved, the combination with a systematic approach to withdrawal can yield much better results. On the one hand, this can significantly increase the company's negotiating power. On the other hand, the company has a "Plan B" for the scenario where the other effort fails.

The *withdrawal* itself can also be related to the aforementioned *termination* option: In addition to the termination of activities in the current jurisdiction, the establishment of activities in the target jurisdiction is necessary for a successful withdrawal or relocation. This topic is addressed in Chap. 7.

With this, we end the description of the options space and move on to the practical aspects of dealing with tactical political risk.

5.4 Selecting the Course of Action

As shown in Fig. 5.3, the choice of option differs depending on whether the loss event is only anticipated (ex ante) or has already occurred (ex post). However, investigating the ex post options for action should not be postponed until the risk materializes. Rather, the company clarifies the question of how it will act in due time, i.e., ex ante. In the following, however, we retain the distinction between the two points in time, ex ante vs. ex post, for reasons of structuring.

5.4.1 Selecting the Course of Action Ex Ante

The procedure corresponds to a classic option valuation: For each option, the expected loss value (see Sect. 4.2) and the costs of implementing the option are assessed. The sum of these corresponds to the total costs relevant for the valuation. These costs are compared with the value added by the operations that are inseparable from the risk. If the value-adding operation continues, the company chooses the option with the lowest total costs, i.e., the lowest sum of expected loss value and implementation costs. If for each of the options 2–5 the total costs exceed the respective value creation, the company should choose the exit option (option 1).

For a *symmetrical risk,* for example, the expected loss value assumes the value 0, while the option "hedge with own risk capital" causes opportunity costs of the capital employed. In addition, there are operational costs in risk management. These costs are compared with those of the other options within the "continued operation" scenario. However, if continued operation is not worthwhile even for the best of these options, the operation is sold or discontinued. Often, it will not be possible to make an exact quantitative assessment, and, on a case-by-case basis, management expertise and intuition will be necessary.

In addition to such a quantitative analysis, indirect and qualitative elements may play a role. For example, exiting a particular activity may change the company's market position or improve or worsen the relationship with the actors in the entire jurisdiction. This is why decisions concerning one risk indirectly affect the assessment of other political risks.

With increasing complexity, game-theoretical aspects can come into play, especially if the company is very important to the jurisdiction or can compete with it in a certain field. We briefly discuss this in the following subsection. Finally, the normative aspects discussed earlier may play a role in the option choice. Figure 5.4 shows an overview of the resulting procedure.

5.4.2 Consideration of the Ex Post Options for Action

In addition to how risk is dealt with before it materializes, the company should also analyze how it will behave in the event of materialization. This means improved, more differentiated preparation.

As explained above, compliance is the default option if the risk is borne in full or to a reduced extent. For the alternatives of dissuading the jurisdiction ex post or leaving the jurisdiction ex post, game-theoretic aspects come into play. This also applies to the options *defend* and *ignore*. For this, we again consider our option tree, Fig. 5.2. Now we are on the lower branch. The first bifurcation in the lower branch distinguishes between the "resolve" and the "ability" dimensions of the jurisdiction to implement the threat. This distinction is essential if the entity decides to go on a confrontational course. This brings us to the following procedure:

1. Comparison of the strength of the company with that of the jurisdiction, differentiated according to the dimensions of "capability" (physi-

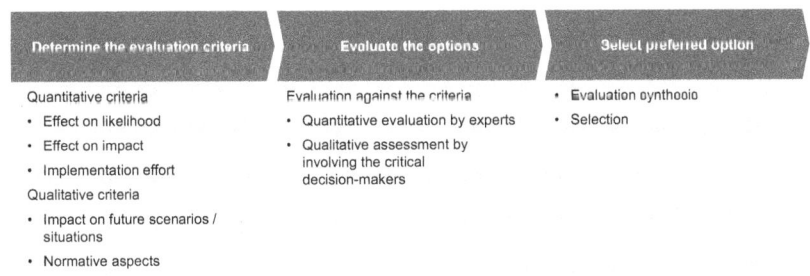

Fig. 5.4 Procedure for option selection

cal potential) as well as "resolve" (determination, approval ratings/ legitimacy, etc.).
2. The next step is taken depending on which dimension the company performs better. This corresponds to the next bifurcation in the options tree.
3. Once the company has identified its preferred "confrontation option" in this way, a more nuanced examination of the jurisdiction's possible responses follows.

Depending on the situation, the company should consider joining forces with partners to improve bargaining power. Finally, approaches can be combined, for example in the sense of a "carrot and stick". This may be in the form of threatening to leave in order to gain concessions from political actors. Once the preferred course of action in the event of loss has been determined, the company can prepare itself accordingly.

To illustrate, we return to two of our familiar examples, which deal with tactical political risk.

> **Example 1: Chemical Company**
> As described in Chap. 4, the company has classified the risk of a 20% electricity price increase within three years as a tactical risk and drafted a simple list of decision points for monitoring it, see Fig. 4.14. To decide how it behaves ex ante, i.e., before the risk materializes, it goes through the decision tree Fig. 5.1. On the one hand, there is no possibility of passing on the risk to a better risk taker. The company classifies the risk as acceptable and finally decides to bear it unchanged (option 3).
>
> In addition, it is already investigating how it should act in the event of materialization: Due to the high implementation costs, it decides not to pursue the "withdrawal" option, such as relocation, divestment, or outsourcing of the affected business unit. This leaves the options of "dissuasion" and "compliance." The company continues to pursue these two options, on the one hand, by reactive lobbying and, on the other hand, by general regulatory management, i.e., preparation for the event of risk materialization. This includes the optimal posture under the potential new conditions. Specifically, the company may already now take certain measures to increase its CO_2 efficiency, e.g., by switching from oil to gas firing, modernizing boilers and switching site heating from gas to heat pumps.

> **Example 3: Commodity Trader**
>
> The risk (a) of tighter financial market regulation is analogous: There is no better risk taker, and the risk is bearable. "Withdrawal" would be too expensive since the impact is low. The company then focuses on trying to influence legislation in its favor and otherwise prepares to meet the future requirements. The new requirements will be implemented ex post.
>
> Option (4), the option of averting the risk, should be considered in more detail regarding risk (c), i.e., sanctions against countries that are enemies of the company's home jurisdiction. A sensible form of this option may be to procure alternative sources of raw materials in countries not at risk from sanctions. The costs of this are low, as it is part of the core business anyway. A contractual commitment to the new sources could cause external costs but, on the other hand, equivalent opportunities. Reducing the risk through lobbying is seen as futile in this case. In turn, by developing alternative sources, the company simultaneously prepares itself for compliance in the event of risk materialization. Ex post, all that remains is implementation by using the new sources and contractual relationships.

In the interest of up-to-date, thorough communication, decisions on how to deal with risks in the company must be documented and communicated to all organizational units concerned. Further implementation aspects relevant to dealing with tactical political risks are discussed briefly below.

5.5 Implementation and Operationalization

The method outlined so far helps the company make decisions about handling tactical political risks. In the following, we will look at how tactical political risk management is embedded in the company and which operational tasks must be considered.

As a starting point, we assume that political risk management is embedded in the company's general risk management, as described, for example, in Hopkin (2018) (Hopkin, 2018). This is obvious in the context of enterprise risk management (ERM). However, even if ERM is not implemented, the responsibility for the management of political and other risks should converge in an appropriate function. In most companies, this function is located at the management level. In very large ones, however, it is often located in a central staff function. Due to this embedding, we will limit ourselves to highlighting the aspects of implementation and operationalization that are specific to political risks.

The effort generated by political risk management clearly depends on whether the company bears such risks at all or has successfully transferred or averted them. In the latter case, the company can focus on closely monitoring political developments in the relevant jurisdictions to identify any new risks at an early stage. As a rule, this should be possible for general risk management. However, if the company is exposed to political risks, specific aspects in the following dimensions should be examined:

1. Implementation by leadership and culture
2. Implementation in the organizational structure
3. Operationalization in processes and IT

5.5.1 Leadership and Culture

The main quality for corporate management and culture regarding political risk management is consistency: Internal contradictions, for example on the question of whether to endorse a particular political measure, can have a direct negative impact on credibility and thus on the company's success vis-à-vis political decision-makers as well as the public sphere. This does not mean that all employees must hold the same political views. However, as soon as they communicate or act on behalf of the company, this should be done without contradicting the formulated ethical principles, i.e., the values of the company. Consistency is key for all the activities related to political risks and in times of high political polarization. Looking at the options for consistent political positioning, we can roughly distinguish between four groups:

1. Many companies choose to *go with the flow*, to take the path of least resistance to political developments. In particular, large companies

aim to compromise in this way with their many shareholders and stakeholders.
2. Other companies, small to large, position themselves as *spearheading* the perceived political mainstream, addressing the "political premium segment."
3. A third group, typically small to mid-sized companies, positions itself as *contrarians*, opposing one or more aspects of the perceived political mainstream.
4. The fourth and possibly largest group of companies—consciously or unconsciously—avoids political positioning. The transition to the first group is fluid. Culturally and psychologically, however, there is a clear contrast between the "follower" of group 1 and the "uninvolved" company of group 4. Companies in group 4 are the most prone to inconsistencies, since they often neglect clarifying their stance.

This positioning affects the selection of the company's course of action. Later, it forms the basis for consistent communication and implementation of that course.

In addition to consistency, organizational governance must be clarified. Here, general risk management often speaks of the *three lines of defense* of risk governance, see, e.g., (Hopkin, 2018):

1. Operational management and internal risk controlling are used to monitor individual risks on an ongoing basis and to implement defined measures if they occur.
2. Central risk management is used for overall monitoring and management of risks.
3. Internal audit is the link between risk management and the top management body.

This concept can also be used for political risk management. Consistency is a specifically important aspect that must be observed in all three lines of defense.

5.5.2 Organizational Structure

In this chapter, we have identified the three specific options for action regarding tactical political risks: compliance, lobbying, and withdrawal. While the other options, such as risk transfer, are covered by general risk management, these specific options may require additional organizational representation. The company can set up separate organizational units for this purpose or establish authority within existing units. Figure 5.5 illustrates a case in which specific units exist for all three types of authority, namely:

- The "Compliance/ESG" unit as the authoritative body for compliance.
- The "Government relations" unit as the authoritative body for dissuasion/lobbying.
- The "Location strategy" unit as the authoritative body for the "withdrawal" option.

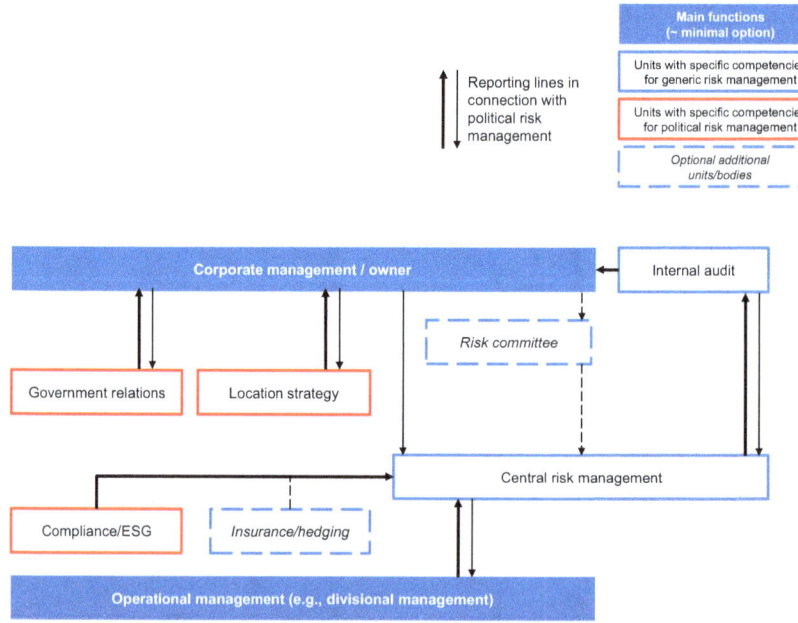

Fig. 5.5 Example of organizational structure

The first two functions are well known, as opposed to the third one. As we will see in Chap. 7, we assume a high value creation potential from geographic flexibilization for many companies. In this case, it may be worthwhile to set up a separate organizational unit. It then plays a role similar to the "Mergers & Acquisitions" function: In both cases, it is a matter of systematically identifying and evaluating fundamental strategic options for action—in the case of "M&A" regarding the investment portfolio, and in the case of "Location strategy" regarding the company's geographical portfolio.

In addition to these specific capabilities necessary for political risk management, the capabilities of general risk management must be reflected in the organization, see Fig. 5.5. For the reasons mentioned, however, we will not go into more detail regarding these.

Side note: The arrangement of the compliance function below central risk management in Fig. 5.5 is deliberately chosen in an unorthodox manner to illustrate that there are various degrees of freedom to design the organizational structure.

5.5.3 Operationalization in Processes and IT

Again, we focus on the specific issues that need to be addressed for political risk management. The additional processes can be derived from the three specific functions presented above: "Compliance/ESG", "Government relations", and "Location strategy". The processes related to the first two of them are described in the literature, see, e.g., (Gelak, 2008; Singh & Bussen, 2015; Schulz, 2020). For the "Location strategy" function, the following top-level processes should be considered:

- *Creating transparency* regarding the political and regulatory situation as well as developments in the relevant jurisdictions.
- Identification of potential *value added* by (partial) relocation to optimal jurisdictions.
- Identification and reduction of existing hurdles regarding *geographic flexibility* of the company.

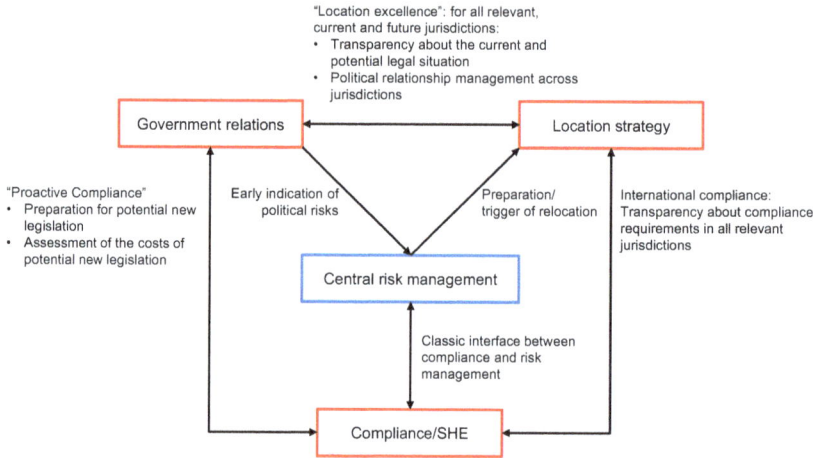

Fig. 5.6 Most important specific processes at the interfaces

The processes at the interfaces between the functions and central risk management are also important. We illustrate these by way of example in Fig. 5.6.

Regarding the operationalization via information technology, we need to consider the diversity of information that political risk management requires. The company may already have a data-centric IT architecture that allows the functions involved to share and process structured and unstructured information. The measures to achieve this, such as building a *data lake* with flexible interfaces and event-driven data flows, are widely covered in the literature, see, e.g., (McComb, 2019).

Supplementary to this, Fig. 5.7 shows an overview of the most important elements to implement tactical political risk management.

Finally, we will briefly examine how our well-known sample companies embed tactical political risk management in their organizations.

> **Example 1: Chemical Company**
> As described above, the company has decided to bear the risk and to conduct a lobbying effort. In addition, the company's compliance management prepares for the case where the risk materializes.

5 Managing Tactical Political Risks

In terms of culture and values, the chemical group opts for *going with the flow*, a positioning that tends to be conducive to lobbying success. The key success factors here are the targeted management of the various legislative levels (e.g., state, region, municipality) and the individual stakeholders, e.g., with the help of the "Power Map" tool. The success factors for compliance do not differ significantly from those of general risk management: On the one hand, a stringent process must be followed, and on the other hand, the responsibilities for the individual process steps must be clarified within the corporate organization.

In terms of organizational structure, the Compliance and Government Relations functions are separated analogous to Fig. 5.5. It is therefore essential for Central Risk Management to be a unifying factor from the Group's perspective and, for example, to examine the qualitative and quantitative impact of new legislative proposals at an early stage. To this end, the company sets up an ad hoc Political Risk Task Force, in which the Group Management and Strategy departments are represented. Central Risk Management assumes the task of convening and informing the task force as required and of preparing the corresponding decision-making process.

Example 3: Commodity Trader

The above-mentioned risk (a) is dealt with analogously to example (1). Risk (c) is dealt with as part of the core trading business, by developing new sources of raw materials and establishing appropriate contractual relationships. The company can provide incentives for those activities, i.e., offer a specific bonus that considers the risk reduction potential of the activities. This can compensate for a possible lower result from trading with the alternative sources.

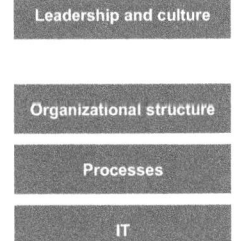

Leadership and culture
- Define goals and measures to achieve them
- Control / monitor the risk management process
- Implement specific measures

Organizational structure
- Embed at all relevant levels, e.g., overall company, business unit, division

Processes
- Define the risk management process, including risk control

IT
- Automate (partial) processes, depending on expediency

Fig. 5.7 Selected generic elements of implementation

> **Conclusion: Summary**
>
> The main findings of this chapter in brief:
> - Political risks are man-made. The company should consider forms of interaction with political actors and not just think reactively.
> - We divide the options for action into the categories "ex ante" and "ex post"; Fig. 5.3 summarizes the options space.
> - Selections from these options are based on both the classic analysis and normative aspects.
> - Implementation takes place by the four classic dimensions—strategy, organizational structure, processes, and IT.

References

DFC. (n.d.). https://www.dfc.gov/, https://www.miga.org/, https://icisa.org/

Gelak, D. (2008). *Lobbying and advocacy: Winning strategies, recommendations, resources, ethics and ongoing compliance for lobbyists and Washington advocates.* Net Inc.

Hopkin, P. (2018). *Fundamentals of risk management: Understanding, evaluating and implementing effective risk management.* Kogan Page Publishers.

ISO. (n.d.). https://www.iso.org/standard/75080.html

McComb, D. (2019). *The data-centric revolution: Restoring sanity to enterprise information systems.* Technics Publications.

Schulz, M. R. (2020). *Compliance Management im Unternehmen: Erfolgsfaktoren und praktische Umsetzung.* Fachmedien Recht und Wirtschaft.

Singh, N., & Bussen, T. J. (2015). *Compliance management: A how-to guide for executives, lawyers, and other compliance professionals.* ABC-CLIO.

Soft Guide. (n.d.). https://www.softguide.de/software/compliance-management

Weimer, D. L. (2000). Review of the nature, estimation, and management of political risk, by J. Monti-Belkaoui & A. Riahi-Belkaoui. *The Journal of Risk and Insurance, 67*(4), 668–670. https://doi.org/10.2307/253856

6

Managing Strategic Political Risks

The enhancement of risk management into a strategic discipline has taken place over the last two decades. Figure 6.1 illustrates the distinction from traditional risk management. In this chapter, general strategic risk management methods are applied to political risks.

In general, the methods described in Chap. 5 can also apply to strategic risks. However, the focus is now on achieving an *added value* when dealing with risk. In a way, this is an extension of the objective of avoiding or reducing risk. It requires a different approach, which typically also results in a broader need for action.

As described in Sect. 4.4, a risk can develop a strategic character for two reasons—due to the magnitude of the impact and due to its influence on the company's strategic position.

> **Important**
>
> In the following, we refer to risks as *type A* risks if they become strategically important due to the magnitude of their impact in that they endanger the company's existence. Risks that in turn become strategically important due to their influence on the company's strategic position are referred to as *type B* risks. In principle, an individual risk can also have both characteristics; it is then both a type A and type B risk.

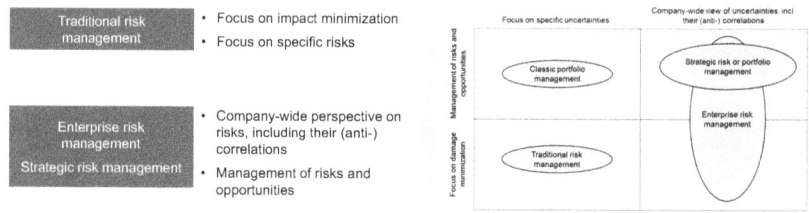

Fig. 6.1 Role of risk management in the company

In Sect. 6.1, we illustrate the relationship between political risks and enterprise value using the analogy of financial options. In Sect. 6.2, we expand the method to identify and build competitive advantages for "Type B" risks. In the best case, the company gains the ability to emerge from a crisis stronger, i.e., with an improved competitive position. In this case, according to N.N. Taleb, it is antifragile [13]. The resulting options for action depend on the corporate strategy. In principle, the options space is unlimited. Of the previously mentioned options for action, lobbying or withdrawal from jurisdiction is included here as strategic measures aimed at securing or generating a strategic success factor. In classic portfolio theory, under certain conditions there is a positive correlation between the risk and the expected return of an investment portfolio.[1] The extent to which this basic idea can be applied to an individual company is discussed in Sect. 6.3. The section thus shows the strategic dimension of *diversifying* political risks.

While the first sections deal with type B strategic political risks, Sect. 6.4 looks at type A risks which endanger the company's existence. For these, the focus is on the potential damage, not the opportunities, which is why the methods of classic risk management apply here. Of the aforementioned options for action, risk transfer and withdrawal from the business activity concerned are the most common.

Section 6.5 describes how the management of strategic political risks fits into the general strategy process. The connection between strategic management of political risks and the strategic leadership process described there also serves as a summary of the methods discussed so far. Finally, we discuss the aspects of organizational implementation and operationalization in Sect. 6.6.

---

[1] Risk-return profile, "efficient frontier".

6.1 Strategic Risks as a Real Option

Type B strategic political risks impact the company's strategic position. In general, they might either reduce or enhance the company's competitive advantages. In strategic risk management, the focus is typically on the upside since the downside has already been treated in traditional risk management. Accordingly, we focus on how these risks can give the company a competitive advantage. This can be an *absolute* advantage, compared to a scenario without the risk. Alternatively, it may only be an advantage *relative* to the company's competition, strengthening its competitive position. In both cases, the strategic focus is on competitive advantages in connection with the risk that the company already has or can establish.

Before we dive deeper into this topic, we want to address an important special case. This is when the company's competitive advantage lies in its ability to react asymmetrically to risk materialization, i.e., when it can limit the damage from an unfavorable development but maximize the benefit from a favorable development. In financial theory, this is referred to as a *real option*. We use two examples to illustrate the form such real options can take.

In the first example, a company is considering investing in a production facility in an unstable jurisdiction. There, it plans to have significantly lower investment requirements and running costs, including taxes and duties, than in a comparatively safe jurisdiction. The political uncertainties would only have an adverse effect on the company, up to and including expropriation of the plant without compensation. However, the company is in a better position than its competitors to anticipate and respond to such developments. It therefore has a relative advantage. It can limit the maximum loss so that the investment in the unstable area has a higher expected value than in the more stable one.

In this context, the enterprise value depends on political developments in the jurisdiction, see Fig. 6.2. We now interpret it as the payoff profile of an option. Specifically, the enterprise value corresponds to the payoff profile resulting from the sale of a call option (short call). The company's ability to react to an adverse political development with certain measures

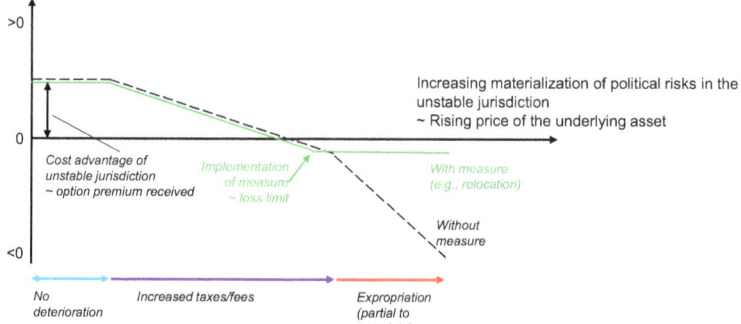

Fig. 6.2 Analogy between payoff profile of a short call option and enterprise value as a function of political development

then corresponds to a loss limit in the payout profile and increases the company's value. For a precise valuation of this kind of a real option, one generally needs the distribution of the likelihood along the incremental scenarios on the x-axis. In practice, it will typically suffice to estimate the likelihoods for the different discrete scenarios.

In the second example, a company is considering early investment in an area whose political framework could improve significantly in the future. Early market entry is a prerequisite for future participation in growth because there are important advantages for early movers, e.g., because of the limited local market size. Early investments, on the other hand, are worthless if the anticipated, favorable political development does not occur. In this case, the enterprise value as a function of the political opportunities corresponds to the payoff profile resulting from the purchase of a call option (long call). The essential point here is that the company can only benefit from a favorable development if it took the risk in the first step. If it could just as well wait and act once the positive development realizes, the causal relationship that is essential for a real option does not apply.

In both examples, the company's ability to respond to future political developments is the central aspect regarding the enterprise value and thus for selecting the course of action. The following section discusses how such competencies can be systematically identified and developed.

6.2 Strategic Competitive Advantages Versus Political Risks

We now describe a method for identifying and developing strategic competitive advantages (SCA) in the context of type B political risks. To do so, we distinguish between two approaches:

I. The first approach examines whether the company has or can establish competitive advantages regarding the identified political risks.
II. The second approach examines the existing competitive advantages from the viewpoint of political risks: Are the competitive advantages at risk or are they perhaps even being strengthened? What can the company do to secure or strengthen the advantages?

Figure 6.3 illustrates these two approaches, which will be detailed below.

6.2.1 Examine Political Risks for Potential Competitive Advantages

This approach follows the well-known procedure in strategic risk management, as described in (Damodaran, 2007). We start from the detailed description of a risk in the Bow-Tie diagram: The horizontal axis of this diagram corresponds to a chronological sequence, from the risk triggers,

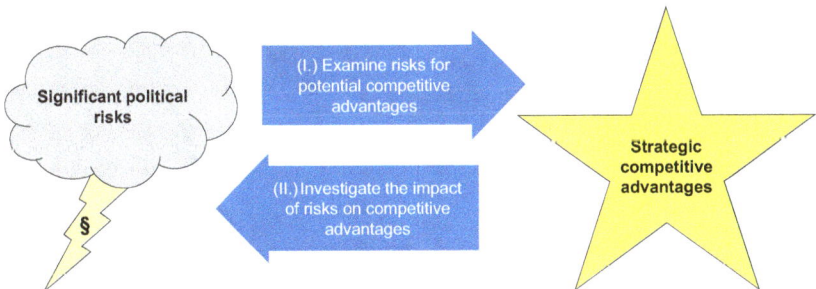

Fig. 6.3 Matching strategic competitive advantages with political risks

including any precautionary or defensive measures taken by the company, via the occurrence of the event, to the mitigation measures and the impact. Using this sequence, the potential competitive advantages can be classified into the following five areas:

- Competitive advantages before the event: risk-bearing capacity (Area 1) and information advantage (area 2).
- Competitive advantages of strategic handling when the event occurs (Area 3).
- Competitive advantages of tactical handling when the event occurs (Area 4).
- Competitive advantages of dealing with risk originators (Area 5).

The first four areas apply to all risk classes, but the fifth is specific to man-made risks, such as political risks. Figure 6.4 illustrates the relationship between the five areas and the Bow-Tie template.

Let's now take a closer look at these areas.

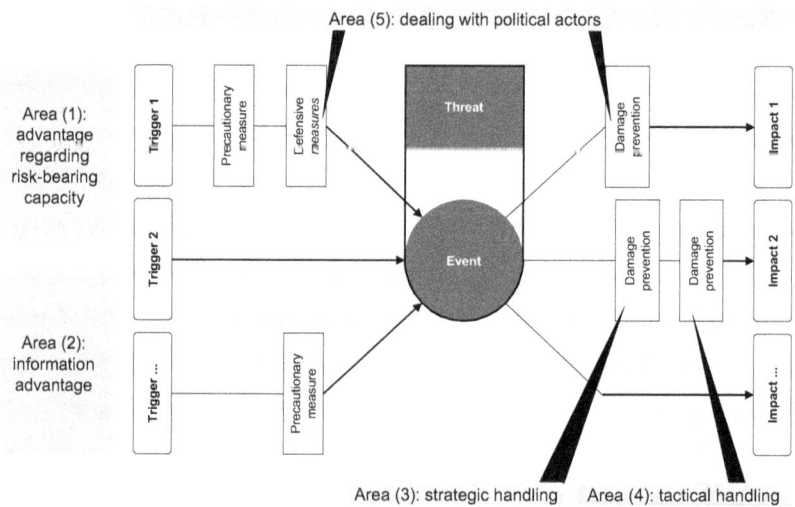

Fig. 6.4 Competitive advantages (SSF) versus "Bow-Tie"

First Area, Competitive Advantages Relating to Risk-Bearing Capacity

The prerequisite for being able to take the risk at all without endangering the existence of the company is sufficient financial security in the event of a loss, i.e., *financial risk-bearing capacity*. The simplest case of a competitive advantage is where the company has a larger capital base than its competitors. Political risks requiring a high level of financial sustainability include all those risks that cause structural breaks in the relevant markets. An important current example is the highly politically determined European energy markets, which are subject to both technological and new geopolitical restrictions.

In *extreme scenarios,* however, other, *non-financial capabilities* also play a role such as where the future of the national currency is uncertain or other parts of the social foundation might erode. Then, what becomes critical is the company's ability to serve its customers' core needs while commanding the resources essential to perform its services. Soft factors, in particular the trust the company enjoys with its counterparties, make an important difference in a crisis. In such scenarios, alternative measures to sustain trust should be considered. As an example, a jurisdiction-independent currency like Bitcoin or precious metals might help in securing trust regarding the payment mechanism. Such considerations amount to a specific kind of stress testing which is equally advisable for the second approach, as we elaborate below.

Second Area, Competitive Advantages Regarding Information

An information advantage can exist both in terms of forecasting—when and in what form the risk will materialize—and in terms of behavior during crisis situations. Experience with previous similar crises can provide important advantages for both aspects. For political risks, access to political insiders also plays an important role. Apart from such in-house experience and networks, information advantages on political risks are usually difficult to obtain. Typically, investments are required to recruit these kinds of experts, to procure the required data, and to develop relevant algorithms. A data-centric IT architecture provides the technical basis for generating and maintaining an information advantage, see, e.g., (Kryvinska & Greguš, 2019).

Third Area, Competitive Advantages in Strategic Handling When the Event Occurs

These are measures planned *ex ante*. One example is the relocation of business activities to a stable region before the onset or at the very beginning of a crisis. Another example is the systematic acquisition and restructuring of companies that have been particularly hard hit by an expected crisis but still have assets that are valuable under the new regime ("Buy when there is blood on the streets."). We can therefore also speak of a proactive approach. The benefit that the company derives from the crisis can be of an absolute or relative nature, see above. To achieve a relative advantage, the company merely needs to perform better than its peers. For political events with a high impact, usually only a relative advantage can be achieved, such as an increase in the share of a shrunken market or a comparatively small reduction in profitability. An absolute benefit, i.e., an immediate increase in the value of the company, can be achieved if the company has proactively positioned itself as a crisis winner and can then realize a growth effect or a profitability increase. If there is a scenario of impending high inflation, for example, a pioneering role in price increases combined with long-term, low-interest debt financing can establish such an absolute competitive advantage.

Fourth Area, Competitive Advantages for Tactical Handling When the Event Occurs

In contrast to the third area, this one is about how the company can optimally *respond* to a political risk that has occurred (*ex post*). Again, specific company experience, e.g., with similar crises in other jurisdictions, can be helpful. In general, characteristics such as flexibility, response speed, and innovative capacity—but also trust, cohesion, and freedom from sabotage—play central roles during a crisis. These are, primarily, organizational and cultural strengths. A competitive advantage in this area typically also creates value in other dimensions, e.g., in the form of low time-to-market or low internal transaction costs. Therefore, investments in these organizational and cultural characteristics are often worthwhile even without the political risk materializing.

Fifth Area, Competitive Advantages for Dealing with Risk Generators

Section 5.2 examines the question of how to deal with the generators of political risks. Compliance, influencing/lobbying, and withdrawal are the three main options. However, in weaker jurisdictions, defense or even ignorance might also be successfully applied. The case is especially relevant where a company enjoys the investment protection of its strong home state in a weaker jurisdiction. Clearly, the individual options can be combined. To gain a strategic advantage, it is essential that the company operate more successfully than its competitors in the chosen options. The size of the company, its importance to the jurisdiction's economy (jobs, tax revenues, important player in a key or flagship industry, etc.), but also specific competencies can contribute to this. This may include a resilient political network or simply a well thought-out, consistent approach to political actors. Broadening the perspective beyond the currently relevant jurisdictions can make a significant contribution in this regard.

Once the existing or potential competitive advantages in the five areas have been identified, it is important to know which of them have strategic relevance. The decisive factor here is, on the one hand, the value creation potential of the competitive advantage and, on the other hand, how long it can be maintained. Less significant competitive advantages or those that exist only in the short term are filtered out in this step. The remaining strategically relevant topics, on the other hand, are incorporated into the corporate strategy. We denote them as *strategic success factors* (SSF). In summary, the practical procedure for this area of work is as follows:

(a) Identification of relevant political risks according to Sect. 4.1.
(b) Analysis of existing or potential competitive advantages in the five areas related to these risks, including stress testing.
(c) Evaluation and selection: Which of these competitive advantages are strategically relevant and should be established or strengthened? → SSF.

Together with the opposite direction of work presented in the next section, we obtain a comprehensive view on the relationship between strategic political risks and competitive advantages.

6.2.2 Investigate the Impact of Political Risks on Existing Competitive Advantages

We now examine the possible impact of political uncertainties on the company's existing competitive advantages. In doing so, we focus on those competitive advantages that have a strategic character, the above-mentioned *strategic success factors*: Strategic success factors (SSF) are specific competencies superior to competitors, for example intellectual property, physical assets, or other characteristics of the company, on which the *long-term success of the company is based*. They serve as fundamental drivers of enterprise value and provide the company with a lasting strategic advantage over its competitors. They can come from all areas of the company such as sales, procurement, production, logistics, or management. SSF on the sales side are also referred to as unique selling propositions (USP). Strategic success factors must be identified and developed. The business canvas framework can be the starting point for this (Osterwalder et al., 2011).

Once the SSF have been identified, they are assessed for sensitivity to political risks and uncertainties. The effects of the risks on the SSF are divided into effects of a detrimental nature and those of a beneficial nature: In line with the basic principle of strategic risk management, strategic success factors can be strengthened in the event of a crisis. Both absolute and relative effects are at work here. However, an SSF can also be permanently weakened by political risks and may even disappear

6 Managing Strategic Political Risks

completely when the risk materializes. The tactical options for averting such a development are outlined above. We now assume that tactical measures have already been analyzed and, where appropriate, implemented. The analysis therefore deals with the strategic risk *remaining after tactical measures*.

Figure 6.5 illustrates the resulting procedure.

In this approach, it is also advisable to perform a *stress test*. For this purpose, we develop extreme scenarios that show a cumulative materialization of the greatest risks. Historical comparisons can help to replace missing expert knowledge about such situations. In Strauss and Howe (2009), for example, the cyclical crises that the USA has faced in its history are vividly described (Strauss & Howe, 2009). According to them, the susceptibility of a society to political crises increases over three generations or 60–70 years until the tension is released in what is known as the Fourth Turning. The analysis of whether and how the company's strategic success factors persist in such a Fourth Turning can complement our work regarding this approach. The effects of such an extreme scenario

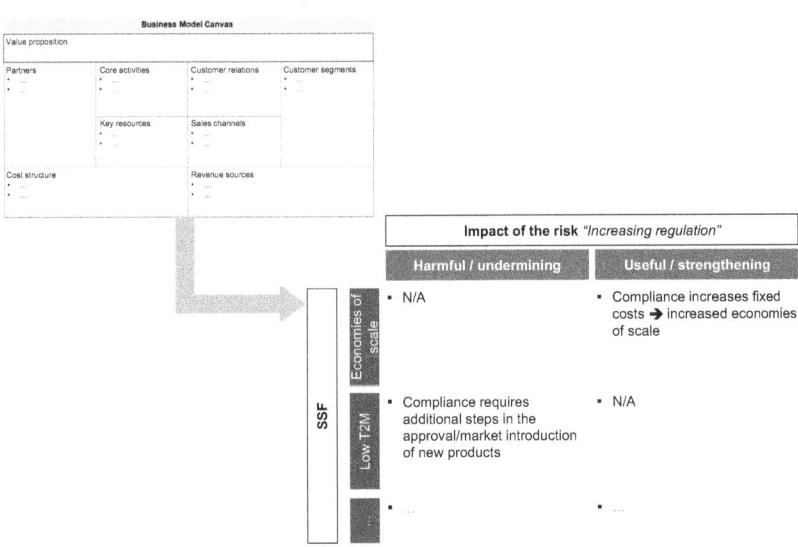

Fig. 6.5 Investigate the impact of political risks on existing competitive advantages

can be illustrated in the template shown in Fig. 6.5 where the extreme scenario replaces the individual risk.

Together with the results of the first approach, we have now assessed the relationship between political risks and the SSF or, more generally, the company's competitive advantages. This can result, e.g., in the following findings:

- An SSF disappears or is significantly weakened if a risk or extreme scenario occurs.
- An existing competitive advantage in connection with political risk can be extended into a new SSF.
- When a certain risk or scenario occurs, it results in a completely new strategic position for the company.

The synthesis of these findings shall be handed over to the general strategy process, where specific measures can be developed.

In summary, the practical procedure for this approach is as follows:

(a) If not already done, identify the company's existing strategic success factors (SSF).
(b) Identify the impact of political risks on the SSF.
(c) Synthesize with the results from the first approach.
(d) Transfer to the corporate strategy → Determine needs for action and implement.

We will now illustrate the procedure using the example companies which face strategic risks.

Example 2: Independent Power Producer

As described in Sect. 4.4, we treat the different risk scenarios for regulating generation technologies as one strategic risk cluster. Based on the current portfolio structure, this cluster offers both opportunities and risks and might therefore be considered as symmetrical.

In the first step, the company analyzes which competitive advantages exist in relation to the risk. As a result, the company notices that it already has a very good information base as well as a broad, deep network with political experts. It therefore has an information advantage over competitors. This advantage relates to area (2) from Fig. 6.4. Analogous to a stock exchange trader whose business model consists of monetizing information advantages, the company identifies two possible behaviors on this basis:

- Behavior as a frontrunner, i.e., anticipation of the upcoming regulation and alignment with it as quickly as possible. The key lever here is investment in generation technologies that will benefit in the future and disinvestment in technologies that will be disadvantaged in the future, at a time when the associated market prices or investment costs do not yet reflect the new regulation.
- Behavior as a contrarian, i.e., taking advantage of any overreactions on the part of competitors, e.g., if they want to sell a technology in a hurry that has recently been put at a regulatory disadvantage and accept a price that is (too) low.

The company now investigates what *additional* capabilities are needed for the two options. It comes to the following conclusion:

- Required capabilities re frontrunner: in particular, the ability to rapidly implement investment and divestment projects, e.g., by partnering with financiers and continuously managing a project pipeline (competence area 3, and in some cases also 4).
- Required capabilities re contrarian:

    - Best-in-class evaluation of generation assets to properly identify opportunities (competence area 2).
    - Robust capital structure and high risk-bearing capacity to be able to handle investments and to survive potential intermediate losses (competence area 1).

The company ultimately opts for the frontrunner option because it already has most of the capabilities required for this. The remaining capability gaps are closed later in the process.

In the second step, the company examines the impact of the risk cluster on existing strategic success factors. The most important SSF at risk is today's broad technology mix, which provides an internal hedge against fluctuations of individual fuel prices. In the event of a ban or prohibitive taxation of certain generation technologies, the company would have to divest them and would lose the internal hedge. The second SSF, economies of scale regarding costs and competencies, on the other hand, would only be indirectly affected. To reduce the threat to the broad technology mix, the company decides to expand geographically into jurisdictions with different energy policies.

In addition to these strategic measures, the company examines which *tactical* activities need to be addressed with regards to Scenarios (B) and (C). The decision tree in Fig. 5.1 is used for this.

Scenario (B) "New focus on national self-sufficiency" with the consequence of a reduction in asset value of 15% within 10 years is so significant that we first ask the question of how to avert the risk. Due to the political relations and an inconsistent public opinion, the company concludes that systematic lobbying is promising. The aim is to keep protectionist measures such as tariffs as low as possible and, in parallel, to obtain exemptions for primary energy sources.

Scenario (C) "New focus on profitability" with a 10% increase in asset value within 20 years clearly represents an opportunity. Nevertheless, the company can use the toolbox to deal with tactical political risks. It again opts for lobbying measures to increase the probability of this scenario occurring.

In sum, this results in a strategy with two lines of defense: The first, a tactical line, consists of influencing political decision-makers. The second, a strategic line, prepares the company for the event that lobbying is not sufficiently successful. The three pillars of this are information advantage, structural flexibility, and jurisdictional/geographic diversification.

Example 3: Commodity Trader

We consider here the two risks classified as strategic: supply chain laws (b) and expropriation of storage facilities (d). In both cases, the risks are completely asymmetric, and the company suffers massive damage if they materialize. The company sees competitive advantages from these risks exclusively in its ability to react quickly when the risk occurs. It has neither an outstanding risk-bearing capacity nor an information advantage regarding political risks. The analysis of the competitive advantages affected by the risks reveals a comprehensive threat from risk (b), which may even threaten the existence of the company. The expropriation of storage facilities, on the other hand, exclusively threatens vertical integration in the affected commodities segment.

As the main option for dealing with both risks, it ultimately identifies "retreat" and, in turn, the ability to relocate the affected sites quickly and cost-effectively if the risks materialize. In detail, this requires the following competencies, equally for both risks:

> - Being able to relocate quickly and efficiently (competence areas 3 and 4).
> - Recognizing early when the risk occurs (competence area 2).
>
> The company addresses the need for action in competence area 2 by systematically developing relevant sources of information.
> We refer to the ability to relocate quickly and efficiently as geographic flexibility. We therefore discuss example 3 in more detail in Chap. 7.

Building up competencies in dealing with a risk can both reduce the risk impact and increase the company's expected return. In the risk-return diagram, see Fig. 3.10, the position of the company or the affected business unit then improves in both dimensions.

In addition, an improvement in the risk-return profile can also be achieved by combining business activities. In the following, we examine this option in more detail.

6.3 Strategic Portfolio Management

We now turn to how the basic idea of risk diversification can be applied to strategic political risks. In Sect. 3.5, we briefly outlined the concept of classical portfolio management. A prerequisite for the method is the ability to quantify the risks. It is therefore typically applied to investments whose historical market prices are available. The trend and volatility of these prices are then used to analyze the (price) risks associated with the investment.

In Sect. 4.2, we discussed the possibilities for assessing political risks. If several such risks are present, it is advisable to form groups of coupled, i.e., of positively or negatively correlated, individual risks. Correlations across such risk clusters are then neglected. Historical market prices are replaced by scenarios concerning the risk clusters to enable a rough risk assessment. The risk clusters are linked to the company's financial indicators via driver trees.

For large companies with a portfolio of activities, a driver tree can be created for each activity. This is also possible for potential new activities, e.g., investments. From the perspective of portfolio theory, each existing or potential activity then corresponds to an "investable" asset whose risk-return profile can be determined using scenario analysis.

A combination of several activities can generate a risk diversification or portfolio effect if their value/cash flows depend differently on the risks. In particular, the combination of activities that benefit from the risk occurrence with those that suffer creates an overall risk reduction in the portfolio. Depending on the data, it may even be possible to determine the optimal portfolio where the composition and relative size of the activities optimize risk-return.

For such an analysis, we can use the procedure and tool described in Appendix B. In the following, we illustrate this method using example (2).

Example 2: Independent Power Producer

The company draws on the driver trees and the scenario analysis from Sect. 4.2. The individual power generation technologies—both the existing technologies and possible additional technologies—represent the investable portfolio items. A driver tree is defined for each technology, which calculates the cash flow from the asset. The political risk scenarios then result in different future cash flows for each generation technology.

The company forms an overall portfolio by a weighted combination of individual assets. The boundary condition for the optimization is the total investable capital. The company runs the scenario analysis for each portfolio, i.e., it calculates the total cash flow of the portfolio for each scenario. This can be done for discrete individual scenarios as well as for probability distributions of scenarios. The latter case amounts to a Monte Carlo simulation based on probability distributions of the scenarios (Strauss & Howe, 2009). In both cases, for each portfolio, this analysis yields the expected cash flow—as a weighted average of the scenarios or alternatively as the cash flow of the reference scenario—as well as the deviation from this expected value. For discrete scenarios, for example, this deviation can be derived from the cash flow difference between the worst and the medium scenario. For continuous scenarios, on the other hand, it can be derived as a multiple of the standard deviation of the probability distribution of the cash flow.

This corresponds to a simplified risk-return analysis according to Markowitz theory. The optimal portfolio can be determined using the given risk scenarios. The difference to the status quo portfolio yields the required investments and disinvestments. In an illiquid market such as for generation technologies, whether an actual investment or divestment takes place clearly depends on the specific opportunities. In practice, it usually suffices to consider the individual scenarios. A Monte Carlo simulation is typically not necessary for evaluating political risks (Otto, 2012).

This concludes our discussion of strategic political risks of type B, and we now turn to type A risks which endanger the company's existence.

6.4 Dealing with Risks that Endanger the Company's Existence

As explained in the introduction to this chapter, we refer to risks that have a strategic character solely based on their impact as *type A risks*. These are risks that endanger the company's continued existence, i.e., risks whose impact exceeds the company's risk-bearing capacity and its risk tolerance. Frahm (2019) shows how these critical levels can be determined (Frahm, 2019). Risks can also belong to the "Type A" and "Type B" categories at the same time: A risk that materially endangers the company can also imply strategically relevant benefits.

Risks that are only type A and have significant likelihood should generally not be borne: The negative impact is not matched by any compensating benefit. The question therefore immediately arises as to whether there is a better risk taker. If there is, e.g., an insurance company, the risk is transferred. Otherwise, it is advisable to avoid the risk, either by withdrawing from the risky business activity or, if possible, by averting the risk. The theory for dealing with such risks is therefore quite simple.

For risks that are simultaneously type A and B and therefore borne by the company, the following additional tasks are necessary:

- In any case, the involvement of the company's top management and owners is required.
- The risk must be monitored continuously.
- At regular intervals, for example as part of the annual strategy process, a review is carried out to determine whether bearing the risk is still justified.
- In addition, there may be regulatory requirements that need to be fulfilled.

Let us take a closer look at such regulatory requirements. For example, Wikipedia describes the legal situation in Germany based on Auditing Standard 340 issued by the Institute of Public Auditors in Germany (IDW).[2] In summary, the required necessary measures have already been dealt with in the previous chapters:

- Determination of risk fields (IDW PS 340.7–8); risk identification and risk analysis (IDW PS 340.9–10): Sects. 4.1 and 4.2.
- Risk communication (IDW PS 340.11–12); assignment of responsibilities and tasks (IDW PS 340.13–14); establishment of a monitoring system (IDW PS 340.15–16): Sect. 4.3.
- Documentation of the measures taken (IDW PS 340.17–18): Sect. 5.4.

When these external requirements are met, it clearly must not lead to giving up entrepreneurial responsibility for the risks. Particularly in corporate groups where management and ownership roles are separated, attention must be paid to this.

In any case, strategic political risks require a high level of attention from top management. To ensure this attention is given, strategic risk management is embedded in the strategic leadership process. We address this topic in the following.

6.5 Integration of Political Risks into the Strategic Leadership Process

The way in which a company finds and implements its strategy has been described extensively (see, e.g., Coenenberg et al., 2015). The activities related to political risks can be assigned to the steps in the classical strategic leadership process. From this perspective, risk management is a subset of strategy development and implementation. Such an assignment is shown in Fig. 6.6. The top of the figure shows a typical strategy process which, after an analysis phase, derives specific measures from the mission statement and main strategic goals in a top-down manner. The activities

---

[2] https://de.wikipedia.org/wiki/IDW_PS_340

6 Managing Strategic Political Risks

	Analysis	Vision/mission/ positioning	Strategic objectives	Measures	Implementation/ control
Activities – examples	• External analysis: PEST, 5 forces • Internal analysis: SWOT	• Vision and rationale of company existence • Mission statement / core values • Positioning and strategic success factors	• Overarching long-term objectives • Specific qualitative and quantitative targets, e.g., market share, growth, margin	• Overarching long-term objectives • Specific qualitative and quantitative targets, e.g., market share, growth, margin	• Implementation of strategic measures • Implementation control
Focus on political risks	Identification & assessment of political uncertainties in the context of PEST Derive political opportunities and risks from SWOT	Compatibility of fundamental values with values of the political environment Review SSF/competitive advantages in light of political risks	Strategic objectives related to political risks, e.g,. building competitive advantages by geographic flexibility	Measures to achieve the objectives related to strategic political risks Measures to avoid/ reduce tactical political risks	Implementation of measures Risk controlling Operational risk management
Gener. RM process	Identifition/ description / Evaluation	Alignment of values: company vs. environment	Identification/awareness of strategic political risks	Selection of course of action	Implementation / Control / monitoring

Fig. 6.6 Strategy process

related to political risks are outlined under "Focus on political risks." The bottom line shows the assignment to the generic risk management process.

In the following, we use the process steps to go into more detail on those activities that are related to political risk management.

6.5.1 Analysis

Political uncertainties play a significant role in both the analysis of the environment (external analysis) and the company's starting position (internal analysis). For example, the political uncertainty driver is found right at the top in one of the leading frameworks for external analysis, PEST. The most widely used framework for internal analysis, SWOT, addresses both potentially value-enhancing and value-reducing trends with the dimensions "Opportunities" and "Threats," which in turn can include political developments.

6.5.2 Vision, Mission Statement, Positioning

This is where the alignment of the company's values with those of the social environment takes place. The analysis of the relationship between the strategic success factors and the strategic political risks discussed above can be embedded in the identification of the target positioning. Ideally, strategic success factors exist that are resilient to political risks or are even strengthened if they occur. Otherwise, such strategic success factors can potentially be built up.

6.5.3 Strategic Goals

Specific objectives related to strategic political risks are part of the company's overall strategic goals. This may involve building capabilities that are essential for managing risks. The exhibit shows geographic flexibility as an example. Another example would be the objective of fundamentally restructuring the company's investment portfolio to shed risks that threaten the company's existence, to take account of the current political climate and to put the company in a favorable position for the anticipated future.

6.5.4 Measures

This involves defining measures that serve to implement the strategic objectives identified above, such as developing and expanding competitive advantages related to political risks or avoiding major risks.

It also includes answering the question of how to deal with tactical political risks that arise from the corporate strategy. In other words, how best to transfer, reduce, and manage risk.

Individual measures can relate to both strategic and tactical aspects. For example, increased lobbying can reduce the likelihood of tactical risks and create a strategically relevant information advantage.

6.5.5 Implementation/Control

During implementation, the measures related to political risks go hand in hand with all others defined in the strategy. Questions such as whether a specific measure is implemented by means of a project or in the line organization, or how implementation success is ensured in terms of scope, budget, and timeframe are dealt with extensively in business management literature. Risk controlling and operational risk management, e.g., the response to a loss event, do not differ fundamentally for political risks. As we have explained, however, the typical cross-functional organizational links of political risk management must be considered. In particular, this can include the functions compliance, lobbying, and location strategy. We expand on this topic in the following section.

6.6 Implementation and Operationalization

The management of strategic political risks, as just described, complements the strategic management of the company. We now want to explore the question of how it can be set up and put into action in organizational terms, in analogy to our explanations for managing tactical political risks.

6.6.1 Leadership and Culture

We have already mentioned the importance of *consistency* between the company's corporate values, culture, and political positioning. For strategic risks, it is also essential that those responsible have sufficient formal and informal authority and influence to make and implement the necessary decisions. The easiest way to achieve this is for top management to take responsibility for strategic political risks. The larger the company, the more senior management will seek information and advice on specific decisions. However, actual delegation of decisions related to strategy should only take place in exceptional cases at most.

The corporate culture should also reflect the aspect that certain risks are consciously borne in order to gain critical competitive advantages.

This should not be confused with the question of general risk appetite. Even a highly risk-averse company may decide to bear a large risk if it has special skills in dealing with it. By contrast, the opposite case—a highly risk-averse company that bears major risks without having the necessary skills to deal with them—does not lead to success in the long term.

Finally, consideration must be given to the fact that there will never be a complete view of all risks; see the comments on "unknown unknowns" in Sect. 3.1. This implies something like a "well-informed, self-confident modesty" regarding the surprises that the future holds.

6.6.2 Organizational Structure

To clarify how strategic management of political risks should be embedded in the organization, we first look at how general strategic risk management is typically set up. There are numerous arguments in favor of bundling this at the top level. For example, Hood (2004), Godfrey (2020), and others argue for a chief risk officer (CRO) position that is personally responsible for the strategic dimension of risk management. The CRO bundles the functions of enterprise risk management as well as traditional risk management (Godfrey et al., 2020; Hood & Nawaz, 2004). For large companies, for example, there are the following three hierarchy levels:

1. CRO/Chief Strategy Officer (CSO).
2. Strategic & enterprise risk manager/traditional risk manager.
3. Executing units, set up as staff or line functions, in particular: Risk Controlling, Insurance, Compliance, Lobbying, etc.

For medium-sized companies, on the other hand, two levels should suffice, which can be included, for example, under the terms "strategic and enterprise-wide risk management" vs. "operational risk controlling/compliance." Finally, in smaller companies, the operational function can often be outsourced to external service providers and the role of strategic risk management is located at the top management level or even at the supervisory body.

The question of how the strategic management of political risks should be set up depends on the importance the company places on them. They can represent the most important class of strategic risks—and thus of value drivers—and in this case justify a separate function or a separate organizational unit. For example, EY proposes a cross-functional bundling of competencies for political risk management (Assets, n.d.). This could, for example, be called "Public Strategy" or "Political Strategy." Such a function would report to the CRO (or CSO) in a large company. If the strategic importance of political risks does not stand out, they are generally assigned to the Strategic Risk Manager mentioned above. If political risks are strategically negligible—and only of tactical relevance—their handling can be assigned to the tactical risk management.

For a company where ownership and management go hand in hand, the question of organizational setup might be of secondary importance. What is more important is what competencies and methods an effective risk management should have. In particular, it is important to avoid risk managers being perceived as obstructionists by the rest of the organization. A risk management function that also focuses on the opportunities presented by uncertainty can overcome this problem. The personal and character attributes of the specific individuals as well as their executive mandate are critical. A "powerless fault-finder" will command less respect than a "powerful partner" who, on the one hand, ensures compliance and, on the other, assists in identifying and overcoming hazards. Rennie (1961) put it as follows (translation by the author) (Rennie, 1961): "To the extent that the risk manager can improve his evaluation methods and reduce uncertainty, he increases the growth potential of the firm. Such a role is more difficult to fill [...] but this is an essential function in the decision-making process of a modern corporation."

6.6.3 Operationalization in Projects, Processes, and IT

Tactical management of political risks is generally embedded in the company's existing processes and organizational structure, see Sect. 5.5.2. The activities, processes, and interfaces involved in strategic risk management, on the other hand, depend entirely on the strategic objectives and measures selected and cannot be answered in general terms.

In the following, we return to our well-known example 2 to illustrate how structural and process organization can be aligned with the chosen strategy in practice.

> **Example 2: Independent Power Producer**
>
> According to Sect. 6.2.2, the company has opted for a strategy with two pillars: (1) influencing political decision-makers as a tactical and immediate measure; (2) positioning itself as a "frontrunner" in order to benefit from both favorable and unfavorable developments relative to the competition. The competencies of information advantage and structural flexibility as well as "jurisdictional diversification" were mentioned above. If we go into further detail, the ability to correctly assess political developments, e.g., in terms of the likelihood and timing of certain projects, also plays an essential role.
>
> Once the required capabilities and characteristics of the company have been identified, the essential activities or processes are derived as follows:
>
> - Continuous collection and regular evaluation of all relevant information, involving, for example, the "Political Relations," "Data Analysis," and "IT" functions; typically, as a process within the line organization.
> - Regular and, if necessary, ad hoc assessment of political developments on the basis of the above-mentioned information by the decision-makers, as a fixed agenda item for the meetings of the Executive Board.
> - The divestment of selected assets in today's risky jurisdictions or the conversion of assets into contractual relationships ("sell and lease back" or "sell and conclude tolling agreement"); the M&A function is responsible for this.
> - Investments in jurisdictions with complementary energy policies, also led by the M&A function.
> - Implementation of the individual measures derived from this; such measures can affect many different functions and are typically managed as projects.
>
> As an alternative, we also touched on companies positioning themselves as *"contrarians."* The companies would then profit from "political hypes" by investing in unpopular products or production processes at low cost and continuing them as long as permitted—or alternatively restructuring and selling them. In that case, the focus is on the following capabilities:
>
> - Risk-bearing capacity: Going against the prevailing opinion requires both financial and mental strength to hold the organization together, on the one hand, and withstand limited loss events, on the other.

- Cost leadership: This is essential for both investments and operations in order to achieve the set objective.
- All the relevant skills concerning acquisition, management, and sale of business units, i.e., M&A, post-merger integration, investment management, etc.

In this example, the activities are typically carried out in projects, be they those aimed at strengthening corporate values, reducing costs, or investments and divestments. Only ongoing investment management and cost controlling run as standard processes in the line organization.

Regarding systems support, we have already pointed out that access to highly diverse information and sources is necessary for political risk management. A data-centric IT architecture is recommended for this. For strategic risks, there is also the fact that the implementation of the measures can affect every area of the company. It makes sense to integrate implementation controlling in connection with political risks into the general strategic implementation controlling. This is where the key performance indicators relevant to success are tracked, on the one hand, and where project progress is tracked, on the other hand. The management of strategic political risks is thus made operational at the interface between corporate strategy and general risk management.

Conclusion: Summary

The most important conclusions concerning the management of strategic political risks at a glance:
- The competitive advantages that the company can build up in connection with political risks can be structured along the time sequence of the risk event and according to its strategic success factors, Sect. 6.2.
- In addition to competitive advantages at the level of individual business units, several business units can also be combined resulting in a strategic advantage regarding political risk. This can be understood with the help of classical portfolio theory, Sect. 6.3.
- Risks threatening the existence of the company which do not simultaneously offer extraordinary opportunities for the company are either transferred, avoided, or averted. However, if the company bears such risks due to their strategic importance, far-reaching regulatory requirements must be met, Sect. 6.4.

- Strategic political risks are recorded and assessed as part of the strategy process; how they are dealt with is incorporated into the strategic objectives and measures, Sect. 6.5.
- The structural and procedural organization of strategic political risk management is based on its significance and the strategic objectives associated with it, Sect. 6.6.

References

Assets. https://assets.ey.com/content/dam/ey-sites/ey-com/en_gl/topics/geo-strategy/ey-political-risk-and-corporate-performance-mapping-impact-final.pdf?download

Coenenberg, A. G., Salfeld, R., & Schultze, W. (2015). *Wertorientierte Unternehmensführung: Vom Strategieentwurf zur Implementierung*. Schäffer-Poeschel.

Damodaran, A. (2007). *Strategic risk taking: A framework for risk management*. Pearson Prentice Hall.

Frahm, G. (2019). *Enterprise Risk Management*, 1. Korr. Auflage, Herausgeber: MBA-Fernstudienprogramm, Koblenz.

Godfrey, P. C., Lauria, E., Bugalla, J., & Narvaez, K. (2020). *Strategic risk management: New tools for competitive advantage in an uncertain age*. Berrett-Koehler Publishers.

Hood, J., & Nawaz, M. S. (2004). Political risk exposure and management in multi-national companies: Is there a role for the corporate risk manager? *Risk Management, 6*(1), 7–18.

Kryvinska, N., & Greguš, M. (Eds.). (2019). *Data-centric business and applications: Evolvements in business information processing and management* (Vol. 2) (Vol. 30). Springer.

Osterwalder, A., Pigneur, Y., Oliveira, M. A. Y., & Ferreira, J. J. P. (2011). Business model generation: A handbook for visionaries, game changers and challengers. *African Journal of Business Management, 5*(7), 22–30.

Otto, M. F. (2012). MANAGEMENT-Steigerung von Transparenz und Qualität in der strategisch-finanziellen Führung. *Energiewirtschaftliche Tagesfragen, 62*(6), 75.

Rennie, R. A. (1961). The measurement of risk. *The Journal of Insurance, 28*(1), 83–91.

Strauss, W., & Howe, N. (2009). *The fourth turning: What the cycles of history tell us about America's next rendezvous with destiny*. Crown.

7

Geographic Flexibility as a Key Strategy in Political Risk Management

The word "firm," i.e., an enterprise, means "solid" in Latin and implies a certain rigidity that characterizes a company. It originates from the fact that (nominal) capital is firmly tied to the organization and separated only in the event of the firm's liquidation. Of course, within that framework, a firm can very well exhibit flexibility. The *flexible enterprise* is mostly understood in terms of organizational flexibility, which enables it to respond quickly and adequately to changing environmental conditions (see, e.g., Volberda, 1999). Raynor (2007), in turn, examines how the firm can achieve strategic flexibility, that is, how flexibility can become a critical competitive advantage. To do so, he focuses on building a portfolio of initiatives that address different strategic scenarios (Raynor, 2007). This approach corresponds to the strategic portfolio management we discussed in Sect. 6.3.

We can regard the company's geographic flexibility as the supreme discipline in dealing with strategic political risks for two reasons: First, flexibility helps avert or drastically reduce the expected damage. At the same time, the company can gain a significant competitive advantage, regardless of whether the risk materializes. In this way, it achieves immediate value creation. The decision in favor of geographic flexibility is then a no-regret move. The potential for value creation is already evident from a simple comparison of international tax burdens. Ceteris paribus, for example, the net profit of a company that moves from a location with 31% effective profit tax (for example Germany) to one with only 12% (most favorable Swiss locations) improves by over 27 percent.

In a sense, the threat triggers the implementation of state-of-the-art competencies and structures. Depending on the size and importance of the company, as well as the size and behavior of the existing or future jurisdiction, it is even possible that the company will go from being a mere command receiver to a negotiating partner on par with the jurisdiction. In conclusion, strategic risks of both types, i.e., risks with a critical impact as well as those that offer a differentiation option, can be managed through this strategy. To achieve geographic flexibility, options come into play that have only been developed in recent decades and years based on digital technologies.

The specific details for departing from a jurisdiction are already covered under the term *relocation*; see, for example, (Shortland, 1987, 1990; Capik & Dej, 2019; Learmonth, 1985). A distinction is made between the relocation of the entire company and of individual divisions or functions, i.e., a partial relocation. Furthermore, a relocation can take place within the current jurisdiction. In this case, the political risks remain unchanged. We therefore focus on cross-jurisdictional relocations. Clearly, a company's relocation to another jurisdiction may be for non-political reasons, such as to strengthen its presence in the dominant sales market or to reduce operational costs. However, political factors—both existing and potential future ones—play a significant, if not the determining, role in most cases.

> **Important**
> In contrast to an actual relocation, our main objective is to *prepare* the company so that a *potential future relocation* is *simplified* as much as possible. This preparation should be largely independent of the concrete new location, to have a broad option space.

For many large corporations, the issue of *site selection* is already well known. They are currently the focus of the OECD BEPS initiative, which covers companies with annual sales of USD 750 million or more. The fact that digital transformation can be a key driver of internationalization has been discussed in detail for some time now (Kotha et al., 2001). This driver is increasingly becoming viable for small and mid-sized enterprises (SME). As mid-sized companies become more flexible, it can be assumed that counter-reactions, such as tax harmonization, will be extended to this segment. For many small companies, a relocation might challenge the customer relationships and thereby the most critical structural element. However, digital communication as well as the trends toward special economic zones and improved data protection favor geographic flexibility.[1] It is possible that these developments will level out or even overcompensate for efforts toward centralization or harmonization. Finally, current geopolitical developments appear to be aggravating the new bloc formation, "Russia/China vs. the West." In the extreme scenario of a world with no trade relations between the two blocs—and no non-aligned states—the options space would be reduced to jurisdictions within a bloc. We do not think this scenario is very likely. Large and economically significant regions are already hedging their bets, such as the Indian subcontinent, the Middle East, or South America.

In any case, geographically flexible companies have an advantage: whether as *early movers* that can change jurisdictions in good time or purely because of the immediate potential for value enhancement. Clearly, geographic flexibility does not come easily to many companies. We want to support a rational decision with the options for action outlined in this chapter. It is possible that a company will not take any action at all, based on this. For the reasons given above, however, we assume that this case will remain the exception rather than the rule.

We start in Sect. 7.1 by illustrating the historical background. We then treat the topic like a strategic project, starting with clarification of the approach and decision path, Sect. 7.2. This is followed by the systematics for flexibilization of the critical assets as well as the corporate and contractual structure, in Sect. 7.3. Subsequently, we discuss the selection of target jurisdictions in Sect. 7.4. In this section, we also continue with our practical example of the commodity trader. This is followed by a

---

[1] The trend towards improved data security is not uniform. Rather, the development can be understood as a continuous competition between data owners and service providers who monetize the data of their customers or comply with governmental requests concerning the data.

consideration of the possible defensive measures that the legacy jurisdiction can take against the company's departure, Sect. 7.5. Such defensive measures themselves represent a political risk that must be managed.

7.1 Historical and Current Context of the Geographically Flexible Company

The geographically flexible company frees itself from unilateral dependency on its home jurisdiction and assumes the role of the jurisdiction's counterparty. Between the two parties, the jurisdiction and company, there can be both cooperation and confrontation. To better understand the implications, it is important to examine the relative power between large companies and states. Several works have already been written on this subject (see, e.g., Strange, 1991; Babic et al., 2017). Direct power, such as the ability to interact successfully based on threats, is available to companies in special cases only. However, by influencing state actors—who in turn have direct means of power at their disposal—they can exercise power indirectly.

The phenomenon of companies interacting as equals with states or subordinate local authorities is by no means as new as it is often portrayed. The Fugger and Medici families were already working as equals with the political leadership of their time before they merged with it. In particular, the Fuggers were active beyond the narrow boundaries of the contemporary feudal jurisdictions. From this perspective, the ongoing wave of globalization represents the analogous development on a larger scale, with both jurisdictions and companies many times larger than the Italian or German dominions of the time. The main drivers of this development are, on the one hand, functional, e.g., locating R&D in an industrialized country, production in an emerging country. On the other hand, the development is driven by tax-related reasons. Then as now, however, most companies are anchored within a jurisdiction and hierarchically subordinated to it.

7 Geographic Flexibility as a Key Strategy in Political Risk...

We can compare the relative strength of companies and jurisdictions to the options for reacting to a cratic threat, as presented in Sect. 5.2. A company that is weak relative to the jurisdiction will typically choose the "compliance" option or, in exceptional cases, remain inactive. At the other end of the scale is the company which can afford to "stand up to the jurisdiction", whether in direct confrontation or by dissuading the state actors from their plan. Between these two poles, the option of geographic flexibility is also available to smaller companies, see Fig. 7.1. Put simply, the size and the geographic flexibility of a company are the essential factors for its relative strength. These factors can certainly be combined. For medium-sized and smaller companies, however, geographic flexibility is usually the only way to change the state of unilateral dependency.

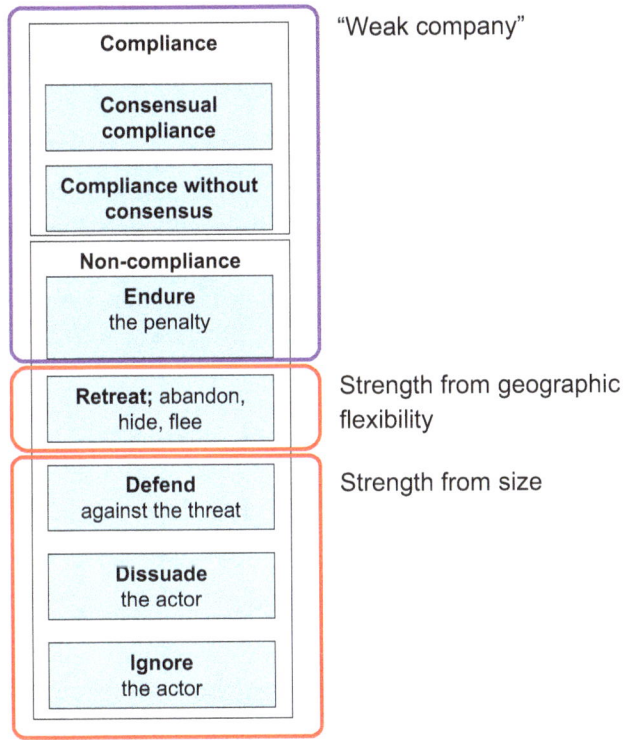

Fig. 7.1 Options depending on the company's relative strength vs. the jurisdiction

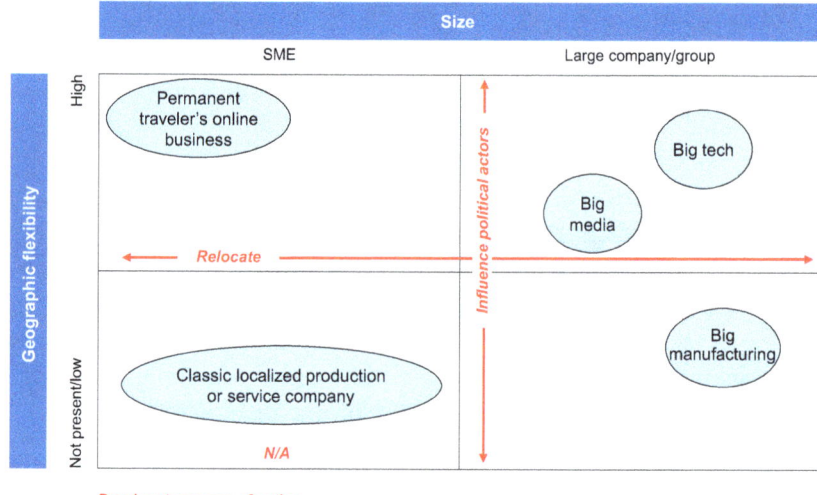

Fig. 7.2 Prototypical companies and dominant courses of action

Figure 7.2 classifies some industries and company types based on these two factors. In terms of relative strength, the leaders are corporations that primarily engage in virtual, location independent value creation, especially *big tech*. *Big Media,* in many cases, is culturally dependent and therefore somewhat weaker. Digital transformation is now increasingly enabling (a) smaller companies and (b) previously non-virtual industries to gain relative strength vis-à-vis the jurisdictions:

(a) An extreme example of small geographically flexible businesses are the *digital nomads* or *permanent travelers*. Typically, they are sole proprietors with an internet-based business model who regularly change their place of residence and thus minimize profit and income taxes.
(b) In general, we can observe an accelerated shift in economic value creation over the past decades from the primary and secondary sectors dominated by physical materials to the predominantly virtual, informational, and personalized tertiary sector. For example, even physical asset-intensive industries such as hospitality, retail or cab services are now dominated by online platforms whose value-added

elements are largely geographically flexible. Another example of this shift is the sell and lease back method, where a company substitutes asset ownership with a mere contract.

In the following, we want to present an effective and efficient method for geographic flexibilization that considers these developments. To do this, we begin by outlining the general approach and the decisions that the company must take at the outset.

7.2 Overview of the Procedure and Decision Path

We describe the general approach to geographic flexibilization in terms of a project in Fig. 7.3. The specific design of this kind of project depends to a large extent on the industry and the specific characteristics of the company.

7.2.1 First Project Phase

The analysis phase primarily serves to prepare the strategic decision. Based on the current risks, the company identifies potential target

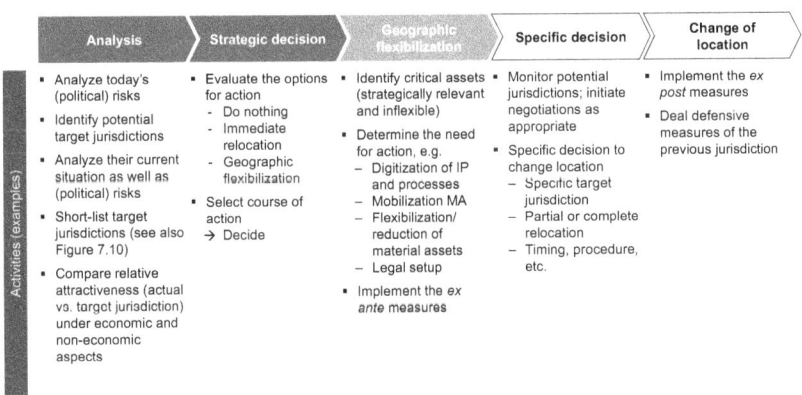

Fig. 7.3 Approach

jurisdictions in the form of a long-list. It collects important data on these jurisdictions, such as the sales market, tax rates, regulatory requirements, labor costs, costs for materials and semi-finished products, etc. In addition, it carries out an assessment of the current and future political situation in the form of a risk analysis. Based on this analysis, it draws up a short-list of the most attractive target jurisdictions. For each of these, a comparison is made with the current location, whereby ethical or emotional factors are also considered in addition to economic factors.

7.2.2 Second Project Phase

On this analytical basis, the company answers the question of whether an *immediate departure* is strategically advisable, see Fig. 7.4. This is the case if, all in all, the departure enables an increase in the value of the company and is also advantageous from an ethical and emotional perspective. In this case, one can speak of exploiting political opportunities. In practice, ethical or emotional factors may be the most important hurdle for a

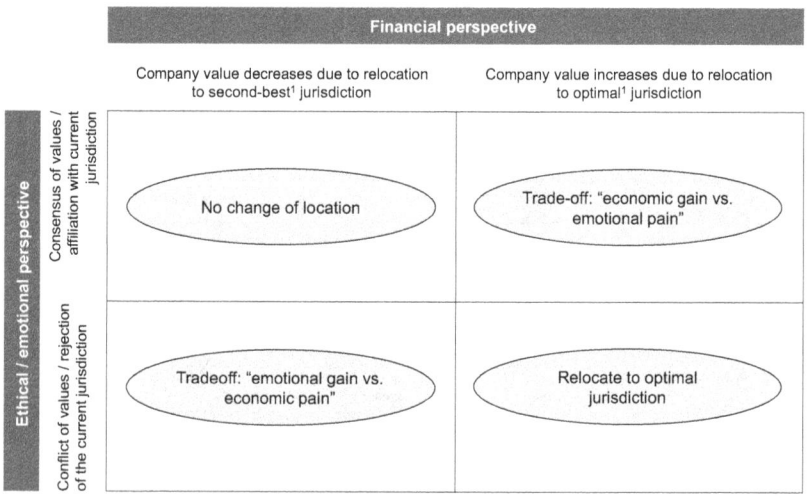

[1] Optimal or second-best: regarding financial, ethical and emotional perspectives

Fig. 7.4 Decision logic pro/contra immediate relocation

move. This is the case where a company fears a loss of reputation or when its management is emotionally attached to the current jurisdiction. Other soft factors can be the personal situation of the decision-makers or a current lack of time.

We will not address in depth how to proceed with an immediate relocation. A starting point for the application-oriented literature on this can be found in (Shortland, 1990). Diverse studies of the motivation, nature, and implementation of relocations can be found, for example, in (Brouwer et al., 2004; Cumming et al., 2009; Rothe & Sarasoja, 2012) or (Haddad et al., 2019). It is important to note, however, that a move to another jurisdiction is also an ideal time to make the company more geographically flexible. This is because the change of location exposes the very weaknesses that could prevent the company from changing jurisdiction again in the future. These can and should be avoided in advance at the new location. Such weaknesses could be:

– Unnecessarily high capital commitment/capital intensity,
– Strong dependence on the skills or know-how of individual employees,
– Lack of transparency regarding business processes or
– Monolithic infrastructure.

If the company decides to remain, for now, at the current location, then the question of geographic flexibilization should be addressed. In the following, we will show how the company may decide on this question using an analogy with option theory. In practice, it is usually not possible to make such precise calculations; however, the basic idea of the real option helps to identify and structure the drivers of the decision.

By flexibilization, the company acquires the real option of reacting in a timely and cost-optimized manner to a deterioration at the current location. Both the deterioration of the situation at the current location and the improvement at the new location can trigger the use of the real option, i.e., the actual change of location. Figure 7.5 shows the analogy between the enterprise value and the payoff profile of an option. The costs of making the company more flexible correspond to the option premium. If the relative situation at the current location deteriorates, the

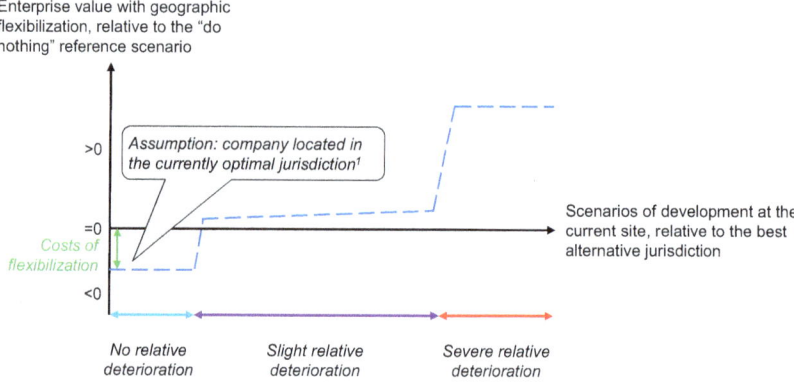

Fig. 7.5 Decision logic pro/contra geographic flexibilization: real option

benefit of the move increases and so does the "payoff". To determine the total value of the real option, one needs to know the likelihood of the scenarios for future trends. The sum of the value added per scenario weighed by these likelihoods, minus the option premium, gives the real option value. If this is positive, geographic flexibility is recommended.

If the measures taken for flexibilization directly add value, this must be deducted from the costs for flexibilization. Examples of direct value-add include focusing the business model on core competencies, reducing redundant activities or generally increasing cost efficiency by automation or digital transformation. The effective option premium can then even change sign. In this case, flexibilization is also recommended if the scenarios for deterioration at the current location are very unlikely.

7.2.3 Third Project Phase

Once the company has taken a positive decision, the next task is to structure the geographic flexibilization. We present the corresponding method in the following section.

7.2.4 Fourth and Fifth Project Phase

The specific activities that are required to relocate depend heavily on the individual case. However, the aspects of selecting the target jurisdiction as well as the possible defensive measures at the current jurisdiction will be discussed in the following sections.

7.3 Geographical Flexibility of Assets

We now show a systematic approach to achieving geographic flexiblity.

> **Important**
> The overarching objective is to *minimize the cost* of changing jurisdictions (Cost of Relocation, CoR) and the *time required to do so* (Time to Relocate, T2R).

In general, we distinguish between *full* and *specific geographic flexibilization*. Full geographic flexibilization considers all areas of the company. Specific geographic flexibilization focuses on those areas that are affected by selected risks. In this case, the company is subdivided into those areas that can be relocated individually. Subdivision into such areas can often happen along the value chain, according to product groups, or along management and support functions.

> **Definition**
> We understand *specific geographic flexibility* as the ability to relocate those *components of value* that are affected by a *specific political risk* to another jurisdiction in a sufficiently short time and at comparatively low cost.
> If the company meets this criterion for *all relevant political risks* in a jurisdiction, it meets the requirements for *general geographic flexibility*.

Depending on the political risks, such a subdivision can take different forms. Grant Thornton (2015), for the objective of tax optimization, outline the following functional areas (Grant Thornton, n.d.):

1. Central Entrepreneur
2. Holding Company
3. Technology Center
4. Shared Services
5. Commissionaire/Distribution Center
6. Toll Manufacturer

Clearly, specific geographic flexibilization can also be the precursor to general flexibilization. There are five fields of action for both specific and general geographic flexibilization, which we will discuss in more detail below.

For this purpose, we divide the current value elements of the company into categories that are already characterized by low or high mobility. At the upper end of this scale is the category of intangible and financial assets, which can ultimately be traced back to information. This is because information is weightless, can be transported at the speed of light, and can easily be duplicated and used several times. Converting tangible goods into intangible ones, e.g., in the form of digitization or algorithmizing, therefore represents an important starting point for flexibilization. These properties of information, on the other hand, give rise to the challenge of ensuring (undivided) ownership. This is particularly critical for information that is essential to the value of the company. Data protection and data security measures can address this challenge.

Immobile physical assets are at the lower end of the scale. As an extreme example, we mention land that may be owned by the company. People, with their limited weight but in principle unlimited potential for value creation, are in the middle of this scale. Their de facto mobility depends not only on financial aspects but, significantly, on ethical and emotional factors, which we have already mentioned in the last section. These three categories—employees, intangible assets, and physical assets—form the starting point of our systematics, which is shown in Fig. 7.6.

At the top level, four fields of action can then be identified for making the assets more flexible: two for moving from the inflexible categories to

7 Geographic Flexibility as a Key Strategy in Political Risk...

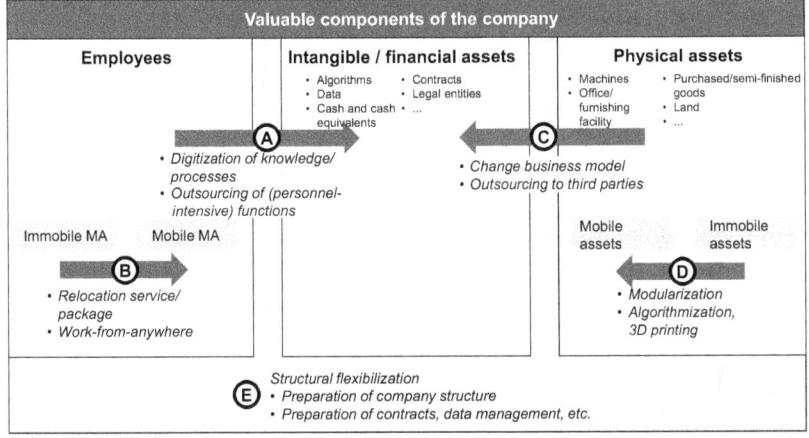

Fig. 7.6 Schematic representation of the method

the flexible one and two for improving flexibility within the categories remaining. The first two concern employees:

A. In theory, the knowledge and skills of employees at all levels can be systematically recorded and thus digitized; in practice, this is only feasible to a limited extent. Furthermore, the company can outsource personnel-intensive functions to a separate company or to a third party, see Sect. 7.3.1.
B. People differ in terms of their geographic mobility, for example due to their family situation. Relocation services and targeted incentives can increase the willingness to move to a new location. However, the possibility of bringing people together in different locations ("work from anywhere") is of high and increasing importance. We discuss this in more detail in Sect. 7.3.2.

Analogous to the employees, there are also two basic fields of action concerning physical assets:

C. By changing the business model, dependence on physical assets might be drastically reduced. In addition, outsourcing goods-intensive processes is also possible, such as by toll manufacturing. More on this in Sect. 7.3.3.
D. Finally, immobile physical assets can be partially modularized, or their structure can be digitally recorded and reproduced in a simplified way at the new location, such as by 3D printing, see Sect. 7.3.4.

In addition to these four asset-oriented fields of action, there is an important fifth one:

E. Cross-asset flexibility of the corporate structure and the contracts, i.e., *structural flexibility*, see Sect. 7.3.5.

We now delve deeper into the study of these fields of action.

7.3.1 Digitize IP and Processes

Intellectual property (IP), as part of the process organization or detached from it, can often be documented, and thus become location-independent information. In contrast, knowledge that cannot be documented, especially knowledge that is only available to individual employees of the company, is tied to its bearers and their possible inertia. This field of action is therefore concerned with detaching IP and processes as far as possible from such individual, especially immobile, employees. In this respect, it is comparable to the objective of reducing personal risk. Documentation and broader distribution of knowledge by systematic knowledge management are the two main levers.

At the beginning of such a project, the company identifies the skills and knowledge with a high-value contribution and insufficient mobility. At the same time, it analyzes the carriers of this knowledge or these skills. The decision-making logic is shown in Fig. 7.7. The second step is then

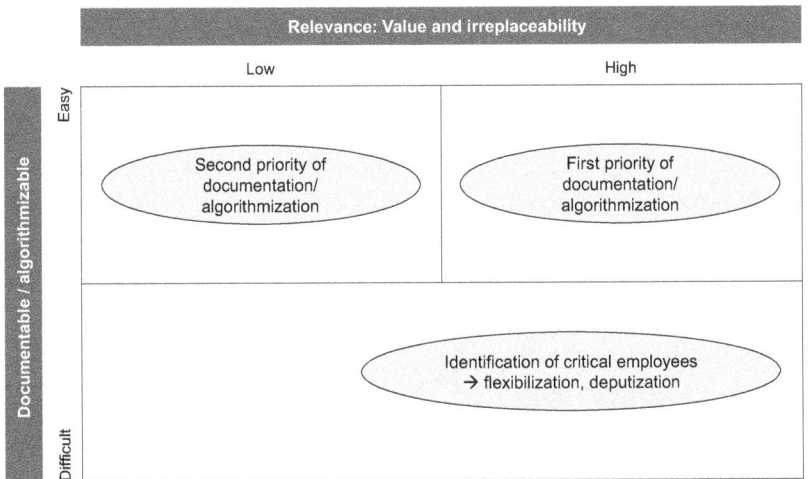

Fig. 7.7 Overview of processes and IP digitization

used to document, algorithmize, or more broadly distribute the methods, knowledge elements, or ways of working.

The possibilities of digital transformation play an increasing role here: manual work processes can be automated, either directly at the interfaces of the IT systems or by digitally imitating the way humans work (robotic process automation). If this is not possible, the process can be documented in classic form and can be used to educate and train the employees at the new location. Simpler or recurring human discovery processes can be replaced by self-learning algorithms (AI, machine learning). The development currently taking place in this area promises further potential. All these methods can have an immediate cost-reducing effect and can also be useful regardless of geographic flexibilization.

In contrast, it is still difficult or impossible to document and digitize the abilities of employees to abstract, link, and utilize their experience from a wide variety of areas. An extreme example is the ability to motivate and train other people; the empathy required for this is a specifically human ability for the time being.

In practice, this field of action should only be used in cases where it offers the most efficient method of flexibilization. Therefore, the theoretical potential for digitizing knowledge and skills is typically not exploited.

Those employees whose skills and knowledge cannot be documented or algorithmized with reasonable effort should ideally continue to work for the company even after the relocation. We discuss this in the following Sect. 7.3.2. If neither of the two options comes into play, the question arises as to whether the company can outsource the respective line of business or even remove it from the business model. The method displayed in Sect. 7.3.3 can be applied analogously using the example of immobile physical assets.

7.3.2 Flexible Employees: Agile Organization, People Mobility, Work from Anywhere

To ensure that employees are available to the company after relocation, there are basically two options to consider: these employees accompany the company on its move, or they work remotely in the future.

The first option has been common practice among multinational corporations for decades and has spawned an entire industry called "relocation services." In addition to monetary incentives ("relocation package") and overcoming administrative hurdles (visa/residence permit, work permit, etc.), soft factors also come into play, such as support with linguistic and cultural integration at the new location or solving problems with the employee's relatives. "Citizenship by investment" may also increase mobility, as it is handled, e.g., by the company Henley and Partners (n.d.).

An interesting example of geographic flexibility in this area is provided by Infosys Technologies, an Indian company that now has over 200,000 employees. Infosys offers various IT-related services to its worldwide customers. Most of its employees are from India. A significant political risk therefore lies in the target countries' regulations of residence and work permits. Infosys has reduced this risk by targeted recruitment of employees with dual citizenship. In addition to Indian citizenship, these employees also have the citizenship of a target country such as Great Britain, which greatly reduces the administrative hurdles for an on-site assignment at the customer's premises. This not only applies to the country of the second citizenship itself but also to those with a free movement agreement.

The other option, working remotely, has recently gained significant importance and acceptance because of the "Covid" restrictions. Technically, it comes into question for all those activities that do not require a physical presence on site, such as professional, administrative, and intellectual services. Even large industrial facilities such as power plants can now often be controlled remotely. For the employer, additional complexity arises when the employee is in another jurisdiction: In Europe, for example, the labor law at the employee's location then applies in principle, although again various exceptions and special regulations exist. In these cases, it is possible to hire the employee as an external service provider—if permissible.

This field of action can also offer value potential independent of political risk management. For example, a company that allows its employees to change their country of residence may gain an advantage in a competitive labor market. Interestingly, the very employees who matter in a digitized enterprise often seem to be mobile (BCG, n.d.). Such employees generally feel that their individual preferences are better reflected in a geographically flexible company.

7.3.3 Reduce Physical Assets in the Business Model or in the Value Chain

It is a major challenge to change the business model of an operational company. Fundamental innovation therefore often comes from new companies. Of the established companies, those that dare to fundamentally change their value proposition or the way it is delivered are often the most successful. In recent decades, digital transformation has played a central role in this. For example, costly or capital-intensive production processes are outsourced while the company focuses on providing a marketing platform: Uber for mobility, AirBNB for hospitality and numerous others. As popular as this model is, it has produced only a few prosperous companies. The strong scale or network effects of platforms mostly create winner-takes-all markets, especially in B2C business models. However, a fundamental strategic analysis of how and why the company exists today should be made regularly in any case. If the company can identify options to reduce or eliminate dependence on immobile physical assets without weakening the business model, this offers an ideal starting point for geographic flexibilization.

If the business model still requires immobile physical assets, outsourcing the corresponding activities to third parties may be an option. An example of this is tolling, where the company supplies raw materials or semi-finished goods to the tolling service provider, who converts them into further processed goods and returns them. The conversion is remunerated as a service; the raw materials or semi-finished goods remain the property of the company. Such a contractual relationship can remain even after a location change. Of course, the costs for the logistics of the goods delivered and returned may increase.

Parting with immovable physical assets in a monetary sense, as in the "sell and lease back" method, can also make sense: In the event of a subsequent change of location, the company must terminate the contract at the old location and find a new contractual partner at the new location (or invest itself). However, it is spared the need to sell or dismantle the old site. This is an obvious option, especially for real estate such as land and buildings.

For these individual measures, increased geographic flexibility typically correlates with the extent of the intervention in today's business model or value chain: In the case of "sell and lease back," the effect is usually small, and it is highest in the case of eliminating immobile goods from the business model.

For this field of action, too, it is necessary to consider what influence the selected measures have in the scenario without a change of location. For example, outsourcing immobile physical assets might reduce the associated costs. On the other hand, outsourcing can also cause additional costs, such as for quality control or logistics. These effects apply even without relocation.

7.3.4 Deal with the Remaining Immobile Physical Assets

As a second option to deal with immobile physical assets, we now describe their conversion into (partially) mobile assets. This option is rarely used purely for risk management because it is capital and time intensive. In addition, various other complexities arise at the time of relocation, such as supply chain realignment. Full-fledged a priori flexibilization is hardly possible with this option.

However, if other objectives are pursued with the flexibilization of immobile physical assets, such as reducing personnel costs or a flexible choice of sales markets, this option can be attractive. Offshoring, i.e., relocation with the main aim of cost reduction, has been an established management practice in various capital- and labor-intensive industries for decades. It is beyond the scope of this book to go into this in detail. However, things such as fully mobile plants enable a flexible choice of sales market. One example of this is power plants on ships, known as power ships, which serve locations with a temporary high demand for electricity.

In addition, it may be possible to divide a larger plant into individual modules that can be shipped in whole or in part to the new location. For example, subdividing a plant can make sense when high-value or company-specific modules can be separated from standard modules. The standard modules would be purchased or rebuilt at the new location, while the other ones would be shipped to the new location.

The simplest systems with low requirements or unspecific properties could ultimately be algorithmized so that it is possible to manufacture them by additive printing (3D printing). In practice, however, this option

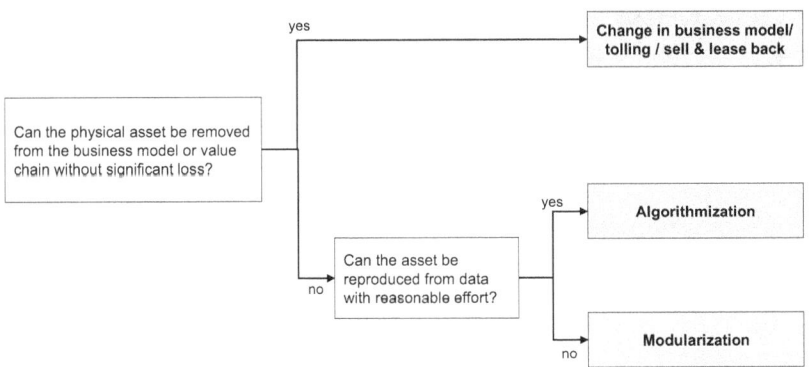

Fig. 7.8 Decision logic regarding physical assets

does not yet play a significant role when it comes to transforming a high value of company-specific physical asset into an informational one.

Figure 7.8 summarizes the decision logic for dealing with immobile physical assets.

We have now explained the four fields of action for the geographic flexibilization of the company's assets. In the following, we will address structural issues.

7.3.5 Structural Flexibilization

Flexibilization of the company's assets usually generates most of the work. However, timely establishment of the required legal structures and contracts is also a benefit when preparing for a change of location. We address this along three aspects: the corporate structure, the contractual relations and value flows, and the data flows and data storage.

Corporate Structure

If the company has already developed a short-list of potential target jurisdictions, it may be advisable to establish legal entities in these jurisdictions (shell companies), especially if the administrative process is lengthy. The assets are transferred to the shell when the company moves to the new location later. However, the shell can also be used for other tasks, such as the conclusion of contracts with local counterparties. Relocation does not necessarily have to take place within a tight timeframe. Rather, the relocation of assets and the corresponding value creation can take place successively. A successive relocation can take place along the functional areas mentioned above. For example, the following sequence could be followed:

1. Commissionaire/Distribution Center
2. Toll Manufacturer
3. Technology Center
4. Shared Services
5. Central Entrepreneur
6. Holding Company

7 Geographic Flexibility as a Key Strategy in Political Risk...

In this way, the company can diversify geographically even without relocating its main production site. Clearly, a geographically diverse company is not necessarily geographically flexible. Diversification is typically not driven by the risk perspective but for the immediate purpose of reducing personnel or tax costs (Grant Thornton, n.d.). Furthermore, with increasing geopolitical conflict, there are additional risks associated with geographic diversification, especially when the company is localized or active across geopolitical fault lines.

Instead of establishing a legal entity, it is also possible to initially open only a branch office that conducts initial explorations. However, this more cost-effective option would then have to be expanded into a full company before the change of location. Accordingly, it is more useful for jurisdictions that have not been given high priority—or if the change of location is a long way off. Figure 7.9 summarizes the resulting decision-making process.

Preparation of Contractual Relations and Value Flows

In principle, the company's valuable contracts can also be regarded as assets. Section 7.3.1 can therefore be read as a starting point for this topic.

First, it is essential to establish transparency about existing contracts and establish uniform, ideally digital, contract management. The second step is to prepare the company's new contractual relationships, divided into contracts with external counterparties and internal contracts. We consider employment contracts as a downstream topic from field of action (B). For internal contracts, on the one hand, the rewrites are in the hands of the company and can be fully completed.

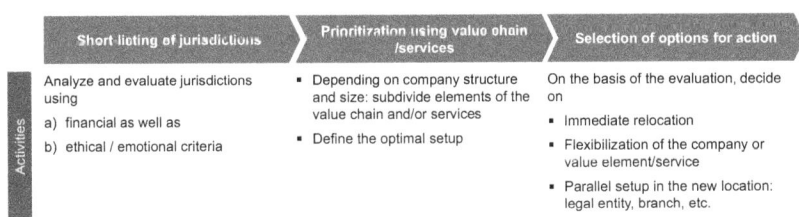

Fig. 7.9 Decision-making process for legal setup

The rewriting of contracts with external counterparties, on the other hand, is more complex. In addition to changes of formalities, the contract's legality and usefulness in the target jurisdiction need to be analyzed. For example, tax or other regulatory aspects may require further changes to the contract. In particular, the current counterparty may no longer be an option at the new location, requiring identification of new counterparties, and negotiations. Of course, the essential topic of customer relationships falls into this domain. For many, mostly small, companies, the hurdle to serve the existing customer base from a new location may be prohibitive. In such a case, a sales function needs to remain in the current jurisdiction.

Furthermore, a change of location can put internal service relationships and value flows to the test. For very large companies or those with a high number of internal transactions, it can be expedient to create an *internal market*. In this construct, all the internal transactions run via one central location. A value flow from national company A to national company B, for example, then first runs from A to the head office (HO) and only then from HO to B. On the downside, we obtain duplicated transactions; on the upside, we may increase transparency and standardization. An internal market may also enable a partial shift of value creation to the head office (e.g., via service fees for the marketplace) and thus a fiscal improvement. In the case of relocation, centralization can then bring other advantages if the new location offers favorable conditions for internal transactions. Standardization of internal contracts may also reduce the complexity of the move.

For the technical implementation of value flows, i.e., monetary transactions, companies used to rely on international banks which operate in both the old and new locations. More recently, currency exchange discounters have entered the market, drastically reducing the corresponding transaction costs. Examples are the banks "Wise" or "Revolut". In addition to traditional banking, the company can use the digital currency Bitcoin, which allows secure transactions at high speed to counterparties around the world. In any case, the applicable regulatory conditions must be considered.

The company should address all these issues and anticipate the need for additional action, when conducting the geographic flexibilization. Depending on how quickly the future change of location is made, it is also advisable to prepare the new contracts and value flows and to identify possible new counterparties.

Again, this field of action offers value potential independent of an actual relocation. Digital contract management, the use of better financial service providers, or the optimization of value flows can serve as examples.

Preparation of Data Flows and Storage

In conclusion, we briefly address the topic of preparing the data flows and data management. The first and most important step is to establish transparency and standards. A data-centric IT architecture, substituting proprietary infrastructure with cloud services, or employing SaaS can increase geographic flexibility. The main advantages are increased transparency and reduced investment costs. However, the disadvantages are more complex data security management and dependence on (oligopolistic) external service providers.

For geographic flexibilization of the company, the aspects of digital transformation outlined in Sects. 7.3.1 and 7.3.3 may be more relevant than the technical design. In any case, the company needs to take a conscious decision on these topics.

With this, we conclude the description of the concept of geographic flexibilization and now turn to the topic of location selection.

7.4 Selection of Target Jurisdictions

When choosing a location, companies classically consider factor costs, supplier and customer relationships, and the tax situation. Here, we will emphasize the aspects that are specific to political risk management.

A structured procedure for selecting the target jurisdiction —or several target jurisdictions—can be derived from the classic M&A process. In both cases, the company starts with a pre-selection of "targets" (acquisition targets vs. target jurisdictions), the long-list, based on quantitative and strategic aspects. In a second step, the company analyzes the items on its long-list in depth to obtain the short-list. For targets on the short-list, finally, additional actions, such as negotiations, are conducted. An M&A

auction where the negotiation aspect plays only a minor role or no role at all corresponds to the situation that an SME will find regarding a strong nation state. A large corporation, on the other hand, can often negotiate at the state level. In the case of special economic zones, this option may also exist for a mid-sized company. These cases correspond more to a *bilateral sale*. Figure 7.10 illustrates the procedure using these analogies. At the bottom of this figure, we make the connection to the general procedure regarding geographic flexibilization as introduced in Fig. 7.3.

When it comes to selecting a target jurisdiction, the current conditions under which the company could operate there as well as the outlook for the future, i.e., the political risks and opportunities, are important. The company shortlists those locations that are currently attractive and offer a high degree of stability or positive prospects regarding political developments.

In principle, the company quantifies the overall impact of relocation on the enterprise value for each location. This includes both revenue and cost aspects, i.e., changes in sales volumes and margins, changes in factor

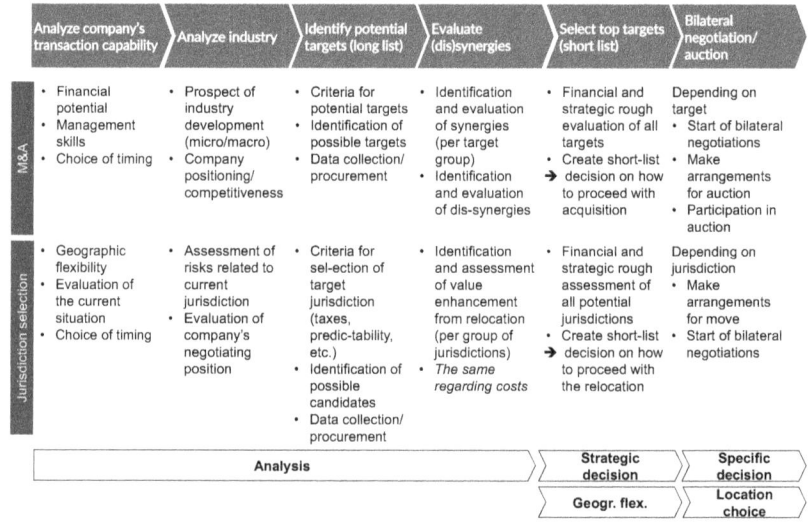

Fig. 7.10 Procedure for selecting the target jurisdiction(s)

costs and tax rates, the costs of the relocation itself, etc. In this, the assessment of political risks follows the methods from Sect. 3.2.

For the long-term perspective, a fundamental analysis of the attractiveness and stability of jurisdictions can also be useful. On the one hand, a geographically flexible organization should be able to promptly avoid adverse developments. On the other hand, each change can result in significant losses. Depending on the business model and the planning horizon of the company, the long term can be highly relevant. We can assess the long-term prospects of a jurisdiction in three dimensions:

1. Range of interventions: scope of the jurisdiction's area of responsibility, i.e., the tasks that the jurisdiction assigns to itself or the share of economic output that it controls directly.
2. Depth of intervention: depth of regulatory intervention in the market and the consistency of this intervention.
3. Switching costs: costs that the company would incur when leaving that jurisdiction.

Company-specific regulations can be neglected for the long-term oriented valuation of jurisdictions since such specifics have a shorter lifespan.

In addition to evaluating a jurisdiction as an isolated entity, the company must also consider relationships between jurisdictions. As is currently demonstrated, geopolitical conflicts can mean that existing contracts between parties in hostile jurisdictions can no longer be honored and business relationships come under pressure or break up. The trend toward "Friendshoring", i.e., focusing on jurisdictions that are allies of the home jurisdiction, considers this (Zerohedge, n.d.). The Global Trade Alert monitors current developments around international trade restrictions (Global Trade Alert, n.d.).

For an initial selection of attractive jurisdictions, the company can often refer to country rankings (Heritage, 2021). Here, we would like to additionally discuss special economic and administrative zones that are playing an increasingly important role from a global perspective. It may come as a surprise that there are so many such zones, with over 3'000 instances worldwide. They exhibit an astonishing heterogeneity in terms of the degree of autonomy from the parent state and economic

Fig. 7.11 Special zones: categories and Adrianople map

attractiveness. The Adrianople Group's "Open Zone Map" provides a comprehensive overview (Adrianople Group, n.d.). The map uses the following categories, see Fig. 7.11:

- Charter cities.
- Diversified special zones.
- Economic reconstruction zones.
- Export economic zones.
- Foreign trade zones.
- Free trade zones.
- Specialized zones.

While most categories focus on special economic conditions, such as lower tariffs or taxes, the concept of *Charter Cities* goes well beyond this. Here, the aim is to achieve the greatest possible autonomy from the parent state to ensure a reliable and efficient legal framework in the long term. An extraterritorial judiciary, i.e., a judiciary that does not reside in the zone and is not intertwined with it, is an important ingredient. The Charter Cities Institute offers a wide range of information on the subject (Charter Cities Institute, n.d.).

7 Geographic Flexibility as a Key Strategy in Political Risk… 157

An interesting special case is *Free Private Cities*, where an explicit contract is concluded between the zone's operator and the citizens and companies settling there. With this contract, the jurisdiction puts itself on an equal footing with citizens and companies. A unilateral change of the rules of the game is excluded as long as the zone exists, thus achieving the maximum degree of security from political risks. In the end, the only risk that remains is that of the parent state intervening, i.e., violating the zone's autonomy status. This innovative concept is currently under development in several locations. For more information, please contact the Free Cities Foundation (Free Cities, n.d.). Comprehensive advice on special zones, classic jurisdictions, and ways to combine their advantages can be provided, for example, by the company "Staatenlos" (Staatenlos, n.d.). Finally, it is worth mentioning the concept of electronic residency or e-residency, which Estonia has successfully established within the EU (E-resident, n.d.).

In the following, we apply the presented method for geographic flexibility to the well-known example (3) of the commodity trading company.

Example 3: Commodity Trader

The company has identified "withdrawal" as the main option for action. This requires the competencies of geographic flexibility as well as early recognition of risk materialization. We have already discussed the second competence in Chap. 6. The focus is now on geographic flexibility.

Specifically, the company has the following objective:

- Overarching: becoming a highly geographically flexible competitor that can continuously optimize locations while minimizing political risks.
- Quantitative subgoals:

    - Reduce costs of relocation (CoR) across business units from approximately 30% of average EBITDA to 15%.
    - Minimize the time to relocate (T2R) from about 3 years to 4 months.

The procedure for achieving this objective is divided into three phases:

1. Analysis: for each location and asset category, i.e., employees, tangible as well as intangible assets: identification and prioritization of the need for action; analysis of possible target jurisdictions.
    In parallel: establishment of the project organization.

2. Implementation of quick wins, i.e., selected measures with low effort, as well as country pilots.
3. Implementation of measures with higher effort; roll-out in the countries.

In the analysis phase, the first step is to take stock of the main assets in the three categories—employees, intangible, and tangible assets—and to assess their degree of mobility, see Fig. 7.12.

The company determines the need for action for each asset class:

- The most immobile assets—the storage facilities—are in comparatively few jurisdictions. The company decides to divest those assets in the most politically volatile jurisdiction as a pilot for possible further steps.
- On the employee side, the company needs to identify those people who are critical to the company's success and at the same time difficult to replace. In personal interviews, their willingness to relocate (repeatedly) as well as possibilities of work from anywhere, in permanent employment or as freelancers, shall be clarified.
- As a third key area of action, the company's contractual relationships need to be examined in more detail. This covers aspects such as contract value (this information is already available for commercial contracts but not for various service contracts), duration and replaceability. For selected contracts that are highly valuable but difficult to replace, alternatives at the possible target locations need to be developed.
- Finally, the company needs to determine which information and algorithms are not yet available independent of location; any gaps here need to be closed promptly.

The individual measures are prioritized using the original risk assessment by roughly estimating the reduction in the impact of the political risks for each measure. The measures are identified and prioritized bottom-up in teams of experts. These teams are expanded into knowledge centers (KC) later in the project. The project management reviews this work and bundles it for the implementation decision.

In addition to analyzing the need for action, the company identifies possible target jurisdictions. At the same time, the project team is set up to implement the identified measures. For this purpose, the company chooses a matrix organization with a cross-site knowledge center (KC) and local teams for implementation in the various countries and jurisdictions.

Finally, the conversion takes place in the third step, where the process described in Fig. 7.13 is continuously revised and refined.

7 Geographic Flexibility as a Key Strategy in Political Risk... 159

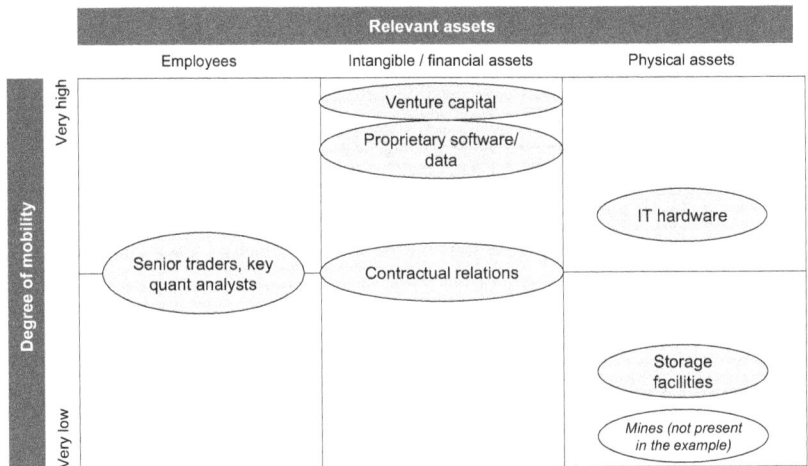

Fig. 7.12 Geographical flexibility of commodity trader: valuation of key assets

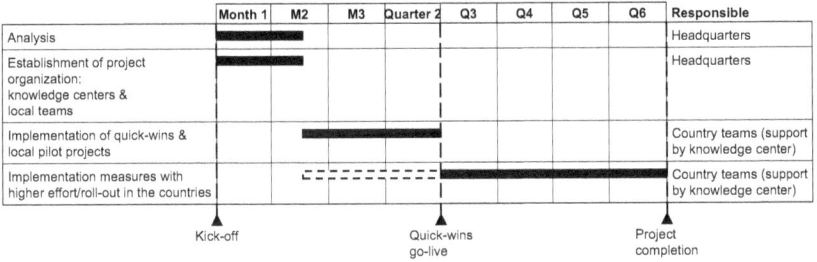

Fig. 7.13 Geographical flexibility of commodity trader: schedule and responsibilities

Many companies face a more difficult starting position in terms of geographic flexibilization than the trading house from our example. In many cases, only a fundamental revision of the business model, as outlined in action field (C), will enable a high degree of flexibility. As long as the political risks in a jurisdiction do not pose a threat to the company's continued existence, a decision in favor of such a restructuring might require additional benefits. Value creation potential that exists already at the current location may play this role.

7.5 Perspective of the Jurisdiction and Its Defensive Measures

From the perspective of a jurisdiction, companies and their employees are customers who contribute taxes and duties on the one hand. On the other hand, they are—potential or actual—beneficiaries who increase the jurisdiction's costs. These revenues minus costs result in a payment balance from the company or individual to the jurisdiction. An economically rational jurisdiction will set the incentives and rules in such a way that individuals and legal entities will settle who are likely to have a positive balance, and so that those already settled will continue to improve their balance or at least not worsen it.

In practice, we can also observe the opposite, i.e., jurisdictions that attract persons and entities with a clearly negative balance, be it to increase the need for government benefits, due to state actors' individual incentives, or for ideological reasons. We can also observe rules and incentives under which a deterioration of the payment balance of the present persons and entities can be expected. There are various other options available to the jurisdiction to increase its spending without gaining value from it. If the jurisdiction does not want to go bankrupt, this will, in the short or long term, increase the burden on the persons with a positive balance, which, ceteris paribus, will increase their pressure to migrate. In such a situation, it may seem economically rational—if not ethically justifiable—for the jurisdiction to raise the barriers to their emigration. Examples include taxation of citizens even after their emigration (USA, Eritrea), special taxes on departure (currently affecting corporations in many countries, e.g., Germany) or even the threat of imprisonment or the death penalty for emigration (GDR).

Ideally, the company can anticipate such developments and take the consequences in good time. Otherwise, it must consider dealing with governmental defensive measures as an additional component of geographic flexibilization. What specifically needs to be done depends on the defensive measure and cannot be described generically. In Germany, for example, exit taxation might be circumvented by changing a corporation to a partnership (Knies, 2013). US taxation of citizens regardless of residency can be avoided by giving up that very citizenship. Depending on the case, it may be more efficient to bear the additional costs.

Further complexity arises when jurisdictions agree to stop competing for individuals and entities with positive payment balances. At the outset, we already mentioned the OECD's Base Erosion and Profit Shifting initiative. This agreement, based on the compliance of sovereign signatory countries, currently covers about 140 of about 190 state jurisdictions. The current focus is on corporations with over $750 million in annual revenue ("pillar two") or $10-20 billion ("pillar one"), which are to be subject to a 15% floor on the profit tax rate. Such large companies may be able to be broken into smaller parts to avoid the regulations. At 15%, the rate is currently quite low. In the future, the threshold for company size can be lowered and the minimum tax raised. However, this will make handling more complex for the states, and the list of participating states could shrink. Effective coordination of all sovereign states would not only be historically unprecedented but also seems highly unlikely in terms of incentive theory. International corporations as full-fledged players on the stage of international relations (Strange 1991) might thus keep significant degrees of freedom.

Ultimately, the "race between value creation and politics" is extended to the international dimension through such projects. In this race, a determined entrepreneurial approach is fundamentally superior to lengthy bureaucratic processes, especially regarding the rapid, effective use of new technologies. The company should make consistent use of this. It is possible that all these developments are symptoms of the current "Fourth Turning", see Strauss and Howe (2009) but possibly also a foretaste of the scenario described by Friedrich Nietzsche (2016):

> Henceforth individuals see only that side of the State which may be useful or injurious to them, and press forward by all means to obtain an influence over it. But this rivalry soon becomes too great; men and parties change too rapidly, and throw each other down again too furiously from the mountain when they have only just succeeded in getting aloft. All the measures which such a Government carries out lack the guarantee

of permanence ; people then fight shy of undertakings which would require the silent growth of future decades or centuries to produce ripe fruit. Nobody henceforth feels any other obligation to a law than to submit for the moment to the power which introduced the law; people immediately set to work, however, to undermine it by a new power, a newly-formed majority. Finally—it may be confidently asserted—the distrust of all government, the insight into the useless and harassing nature of these short-winded struggles, must drive men to an entirely new resolution: to the abrogation of the conception of the State and the abolition of the contrast of "private and public." Private concerns gradually absorb the business of the State; even the toughest residue which is left over from the old work of governing (the business, for instance, which is meant to protect private persons from private persons) will at last some day be managed by private enterprise. The neglect, decline, and death of the State, the liberation of the private person (I am careful not to say the individual), are the consequences of the democratic conception of the State; that is its mission. When it has accomplished its task,—which, like everything human, involves much rationality and irrationality,—and when all relapses into the old malady have been overcome, then a new leaf in the story-book of humanity will be unrolled, on which readers will find all kinds of strange tales and perhaps also some amount of good.

> **Conclusion: Summary**
> In the following, we briefly summarize the main findings of this chapter:
> - Geographically flexible companies are on the rise worldwide. Current geopolitical developments may both hinder and drive this development.
> - Figure 7.3 shows an overview of the procedure for obtaining geographic flexibility.
> - There are a total of five fields of action, four of which focus on the company's assets, see Fig. 7.6.
> - The selection of target jurisdictions should be comprehensive and systematic, see Fig. 7.10.
> - The company should also consider the perspective of the current home jurisdiction as well as its possible defenses to prevent negative surprises, see Sect. 7.5.

References

Adrianople Group. https://www.adrianoplegroup.com/zonemap/about
Babic, M., Fichtner, J., & Heemskerk, E. M. (2017). States versus corporations: Rethinking the power of business in international politics. *The International Spectator, 52*(4), 20–43.
BCG. (n.d.). https://www.bcg.com/publications/2019/decoding-digital-talent
Brouwer, A. E., Mariotti, I., & Van Ommeren, J. N. (2004). The firm relocation decision: An empirical investigation. *The Annals of Regional Science, 38*(2), 335–347.
Capik, P., & Dej, M. (2019). *Relocation of economic activity*. Springer.
Charter Cities Institute. https://chartercitiesinstitute.org/
Cumming, D., Fleming, G., & Schwienbacher, A. (2009). Corporate relocation in venture capital finance. *Entrepreneurship Theory and Practice, 33*(5), 1121–1155.
E-resident. https://www.e-resident.gov.ee/
Free Cities. www.free-cities.org
Global Trade Alert. https://www.globaltradealert.org/
Grant Thornton. (n.d.). https://www.grantthornton.global/globalassets/1.-member-firms/global/insights/article-pdfs/2015/advisory/a-global-guide-to-business-relocation_final4.pdf
Haddad, M. J. M., Sanders, D., & Tewkesbury, G. (2019). Selecting a discrete Multiple Criteria Decision Making method to decide on a corporate relocation. *Archives of Business Research, 7*(5), 48–67.
Henley. https://www.henleyglobal.com
Heritage. https://www.heritage.org/index/; bis 2021 auch https://en.wikipedia.org/wiki/Ease_of_doing_business_index
Knies, J. T. (2013). Die Wegzugsbesteuerung–§ 6 AStG. In *Internationales Ertragsteuerrecht* (pp. 79–89). Springer Gabler.
Kotha, S., Rindova, V. P., & Rothaermel, F. T. (2001). Assets and actions: Firm-specific factors in the internationalization of US Internet firms. *Journal of International Business Studies, 32*(4), 769–791.
Learmonth, S. I. (1985). The corporate relocation: Effects, issues and developments – a review and analysis (Doctoral dissertation, Concordia University.).
Nietzsche, F. (2016). *Menschliches, Allzumenschliches: ein Buch für freie Geister*. https://en.wikisource.org/wiki/Human_All-Too-Human.
Raynor, M. E. (2007). The strategy paradox: Why committing to success leads to failure (and what to do about it). *Currency*.

Rothe, P., & Sarasoja, A. (2012). Corporate relocation decision making-is there method in the madness. In *American Real Estate Society 28th Annual Meeting.*

Shortland, S. M. (1987). *Managing relocation.* Springer.

Shortland, S. (1990). *Relocation: A practical guide.* Institute of Personnel Management.

Staatenlos. https://staatenlos.ch/

Strange, S. (1991). Big Business and the State. *Millennium, 20*(2), 245–250.

Strauss, W., & Howe, N. (2009). *The fourth turning: What the cycles of history tell us about America's next rendezvous with destiny.* Crown.

Volberda, H. W. (1999). *Building the flexible firm: How to remain competitive.* Oxford University Press.

Zerohedge. https://www.zerohedge.com/economics/friendshoring-trend-sees-companies-moving-ops-dodge-tensions-and-trade-wars

8

Concluding Remarks

As noted at the outset, this book aims to sensitize corporate decision-makers in developed countries to political risks, to provide them with the tools to deal with them in their operations, and to identify strategic options with which the company can identify opportunities to use the risks to create value. In line with this objective, we are now drawing a conclusion.

We summarize the most important tools for managing political risks in Fig. 8.1:

1. The first step is to identify, describe, and assess the risks. It is helpful to organize the risks according to the company's financial value drivers right from the start. This facilitates their subsequent evaluation using driver trees and scenarios. Finally, the risk matrix is used to prepare the decision to deal with the risks.
2. This decision separates strategic and tactical risks at the highest level. For strategic risks, the question is whether or how a competitive advantage can be secured or expanded in dealing with the risk. For

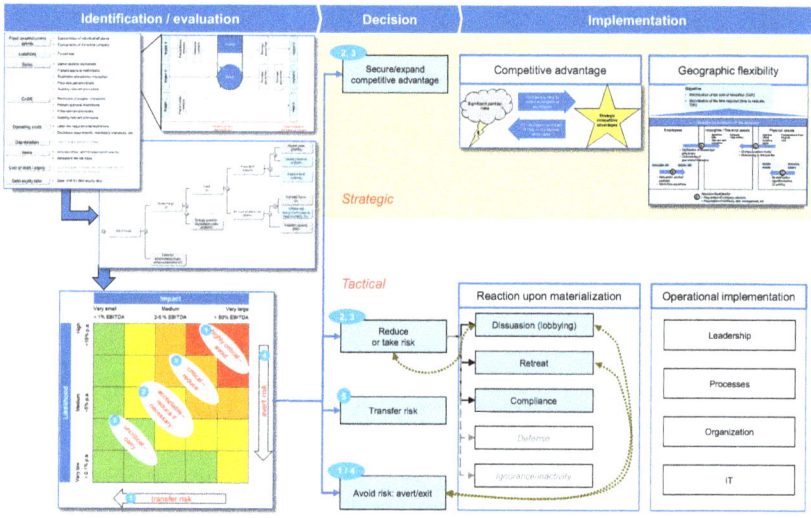

Fig. 8.1 Political risk management toolkit

tactical risks, the question is whether the risk can be sensibly transferred or avoided; the remaining risks may be reduced and borne.
3. The distinction between strategic and tactical risks continues during implementation. For strategic risks, making the company geographically flexible is often the silver bullet.

When a tactical political risk materializes and the company continues to carry it, its response typically takes the form of compliance, i.e., meeting the new political requirement. For operational management of all risks, the dimensions of leadership, process and organizational structure and IT must be considered.

Using these tools, we highlighted the following issues in particular:

- A method for comprehensively identifying political risks and for structuring them in line with the financial value drivers of the company.
- Quantitative assessment of such risks, considering the inherent fuzziness of political issues.

8 Concluding Remarks

- The comprehensive overview of ways to manage risks, both before they materialize and after.
- The way strategic opportunities can be discovered and managed in conjunction with political risks.

As stated several times in this book, systematic management of political risks in industrialized nations is still in its infancy. It is to be expected that the topic will develop further as political crises continue in traditional jurisdictions; developments are currently clearly pointing in this direction. In this respect, we would like to conclude by addressing the question of which directions we see for deepening the topic:

1. A quantitative historical analysis of the consequences of political risks that have occurred for different industries and geographies might reveal certain regularities, such as the cyclicality postulated by Strauss and Howe (2009).
2. In general, there are many possibilities to deepen the economic analysis of the impact and likelihood of political risks.
3. From a business perspective, it is important to compile a broad range of information on the situation and development scenarios in the world's various jurisdictions. Together with a systematic investigation of political risk drivers, it may then be possible to develop a robust tool for determining risk likelihoods. The information could be structured into an "industry-jurisdiction matrix" that provides an overview of the existing political conditions and the main risks for each jurisdiction and industry.
4. Understanding the remaining political risks in the special zones described in Sect. 7.4 is of particular interest when searching for means to reduce such risks in general.

The author welcomes further suggestions and is pleased to hear about specific initiatives that work towards the goal of reducing the damaging effects of political risks.

Reference

Strauss, W., & Howe, N. (2009). *The fourth turning: What the cycles of history tell us about America's next rendezvous with destiny*. Crown.

Appendix A: Taxonomy of Human Actions

This appendix is an in-depth analysis of human actions and thus forms the basis for understanding the behavior of contemporary jurisdictions. It is related to Sects. 2.2, 5.4.2 and 7.5. The result of this analysis is a taxonomy with five categories that emerge from a tree with four bifurcations, see Fig. A.1. Taghizadegan and Otto (2015) describe this in detail (Taghizadegan & Otto, 2015).

1. People as social beings can direct a specific action toward other people or only toward themselves. We call actions toward other persons social and actions toward themselves *autistic actions*, without referring to the psychological makeup of the actor.[1]
2. Among social actions we distinguish those actions that are purposefully directed toward the counterparty, i.e., that are intended to cause the other party a benefit or harm, from those where the other party is a means to an end. We call the first kind of social actions *unilateral harm or benefit,* because the actor acts unilaterally.

---

[1] Boulding, K. E. (1963). Towards a pure theory of threat systems. *The American Economic Review, 53*(2), 424–434.

Appendix A: Taxonomy of Human Actions

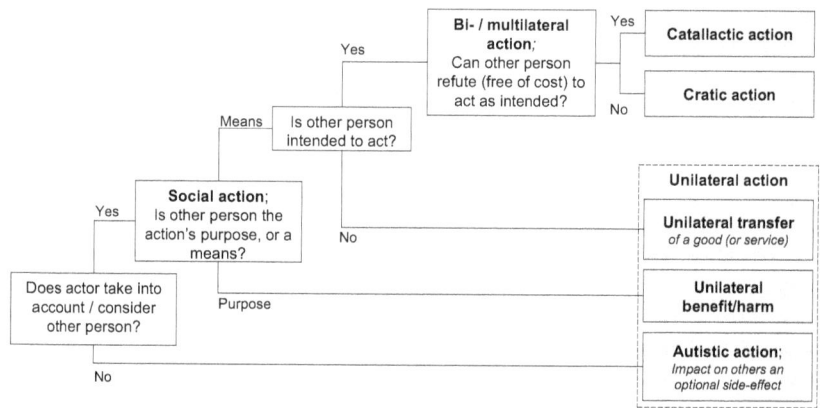

Fig. A.1 Taxonomy of human actions

3. For actions where the counterparty is a means to an end, we further distinguish as to whether the counterparty should remain passive or become active. A passive counterparty that is a means to an end is present, for example, in the case of theft. Here, the actor intends to steal an object of value from the counterparty. However, the actor intends that the counterparty does not notice this and remains passive. The counterparty is thus a means to the end of enriching the actor. We generally refer to such actions as *unilateral transfers*.

4. On the other hand, as soon as the actor wants the counterparty to act, we speak of a *bilateral action* to which both the proactive actor and his counterparty contribute. Here again, a distinction can be made between whether the counterparty is induced to act by a threat of harm or by the promise of value, in the sense of the well-known dualism of a "carrot or stick." In the case of a threat, the counterparty expects harm if it is inactive, whereas in the case of a promise of value, it remains in the same state if it does not act. In line with the Austrian school of economics, we speak of *cratic actions* in the case of a threat, and *catallactic* in the case of a promise of value.

Cratic actions are based on the power of the agent over the counterparty. Catallactic actions, on the other hand, are based on the agent's wealth, a part of which he offers to the other party in exchange.

While unilateral harm or benefit presupposes a substantial interest of the actor in the other party, this is not the case with unilateral transfer, cratic and catallactic actions. Therefore, these three forms of action are also used by people unknown to each other. Therefore, they are of great importance in our society, which relies on the large-scale division of labor. Social orders basically strive to prevent the value-reducing action types of unilateral damage, unilateral transfer as well as cratic action. Destruction, theft, robbery, and extortion are therefore punishable. A person or institution, such as princes and kings or today's nation states, is always responsible for maintaining order. On a fixed territory, their word or law is to apply, and criminals must expect punishment. In this way, they perform a service that is essential for the inhabitants, namely the establishment of legal certainty.

The resources for this service, however, are universally acquired through cratic actions, such as the collection of taxes under threat of penalties.

As long as the service enjoys the universal consent of all counterparties—whether explicitly in the sense of a mutual contract or even tacitly—it is not a cratic threat. With the complexity of today's regulations, which consider a wide variety of individual interests, it must be assumed, however, that universal tacit consent represents a special case.

> **Important**
>
> In this respect, political activities can be regarded as *institutionalized cratic actions*. This results in an ethical circular reference, see Fig. A.2.

Side note: Theoretically, a state could also carry out a unilateral transfer vis-à-vis its inhabitants. In practice, this does not happen, since for the state it is much easier to reach its goal by a threat than by secretly taking possession of the good in question.

To sum up, it can be ascertained that unilateral changes of the rules of the game by politicians or the state represent a violation of a fundamental principle of law as well as the *Golden Rule*, which are supposed to be protected precisely by the institution of the state. Proposals on how this

Appendix A: Taxonomy of Human Actions

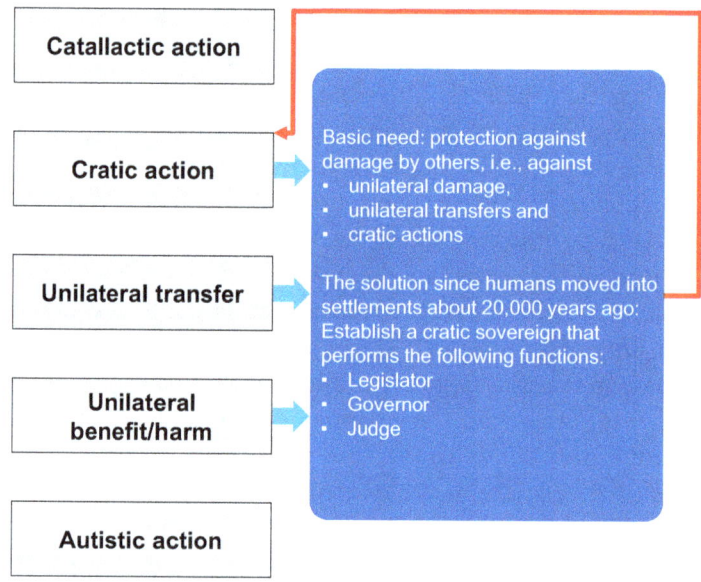

Fig. A.2 Circular reference of the cratic solution to legal certainty

internal contradiction could be resolved can be found in Friedman (1989) and Gebel (2018), among others (Friedman, 1989, 2015; Gebel, 2018).

Appendix B: Tool to Support Scenario Analysis

In the following, we outline the functionality of the *Strategic Portfolio Analysis* (SPA) tool, which is used to quantify risks according to Fig. 4.8 and to evaluate strategic options for action according to Sect. 6.3. The tool was developed in MATLAB by Günter Kneisel and Christoph Seja at The Advisory House AG and is available as a desktop application.

We explain how the tool can support the procedure described in Sect. 4.2.

1. Risk identification is initially performed outside the tool.
2. The company or its portfolio items are modeled using one or more driver trees. The tool provides an input screen for this purpose, see Fig. B.1. Various typical driver trees, including their parameter types and risk drivers, have already been defined for energy industry assets. To show the development of the risk drivers over time, they are set up as time series. Different scenarios then correspond to different time

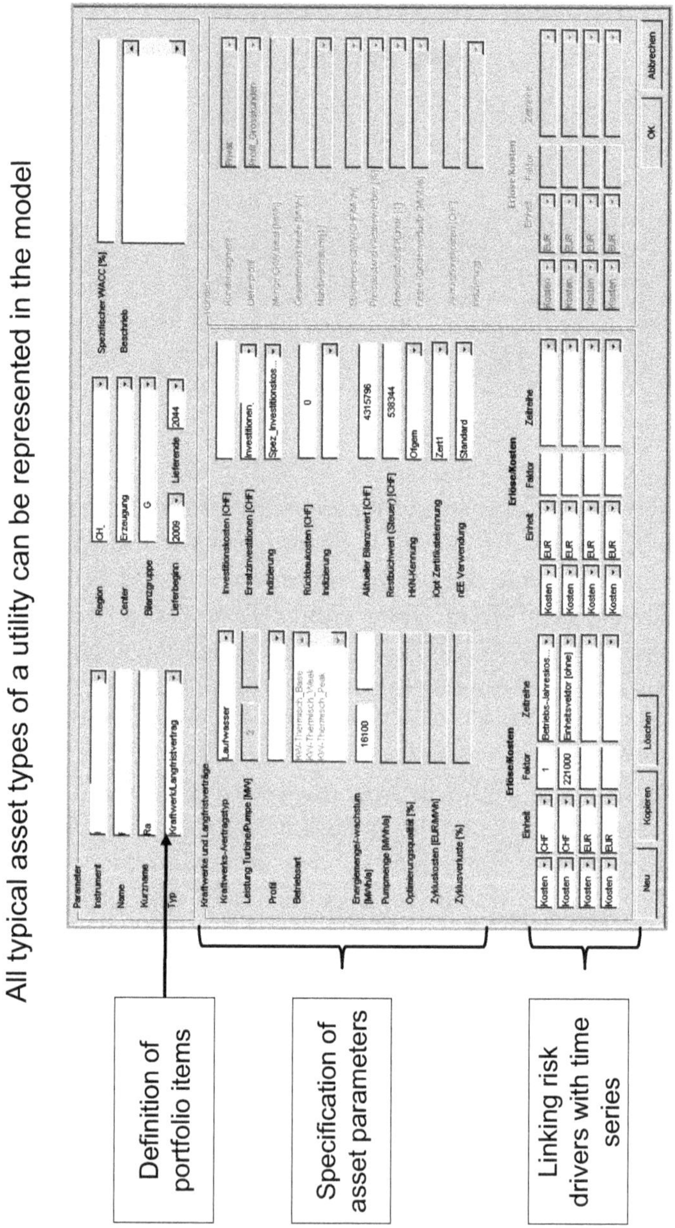

Fig. B.1 Illustration of driver trees

series, which can be defined in another form or uploaded from a csv file.

For other assets, any driver tree can be entered using the appropriate cash flow formula. In this case, the secure parameters are written permanently into the formula; the risk drivers are entered as variables that refer to the freely definable time series.

In addition, different weighted combinations of these portfolio items can be recorded in the tool, see Fig. B.2. This makes it possible to analyze the different strategic positions of the company that can be achieved by investments or divestments. The relocation of a company to another jurisdiction can also be summarized as a disinvestment of assets at the old location plus a corresponding investment at the new location.

1. The formation of the risk clusters is again a human, intellectual effort, and the risk clusters are recorded in the tool together with step (4).
2. The defined groups of scenarios are recorded based on their effects on the risk variables, i.e., a freely definable time series for each risk driver. The weighting with likelihood values per scenario group can also be entered here.
3. The evaluation is finally automated in the tool: for all scenario combinations as well as all strategic portfolio combinations, the typical KPI are determined (cash flows, investments, NPV, NPV@Risk, capital employed, EBITDA, EBIT, ROI, IRR, EVA). The result is also shown in a risk-return diagram, with the defined portfolio combinations each representing a data point.

Finally, the tool can be used to determine the company's Efficient Frontier

This efficiently supports the assessment of political risks and the analysis of strategic options for action (Fig. B.3).

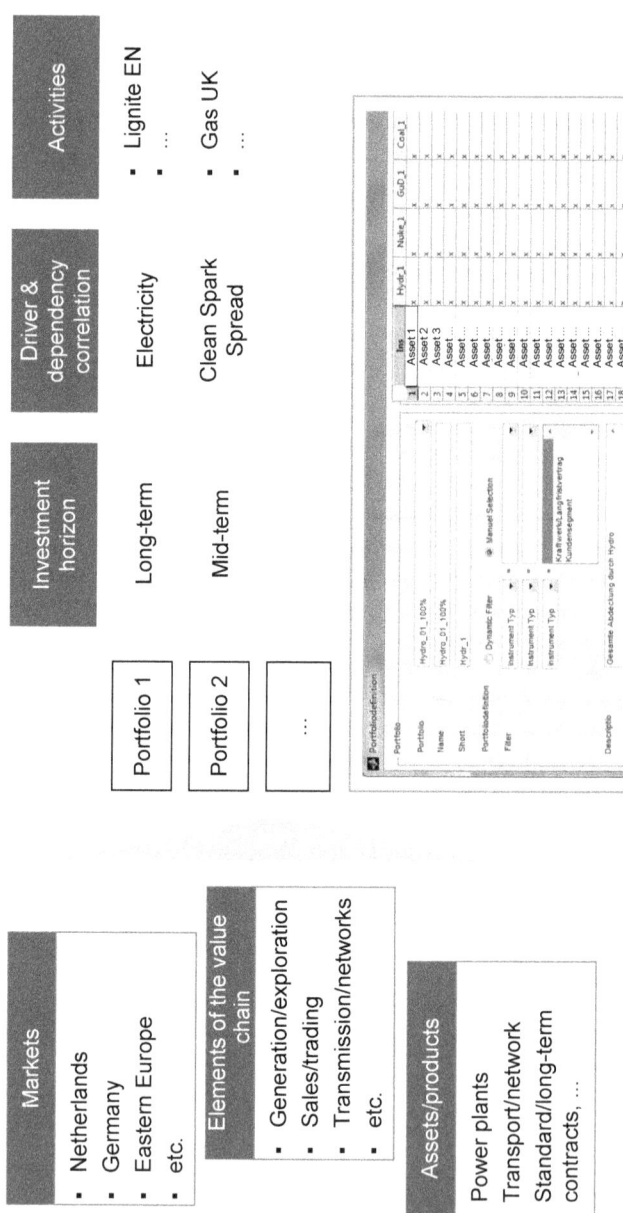

Fig. B.2 Definition of the asset portfolios

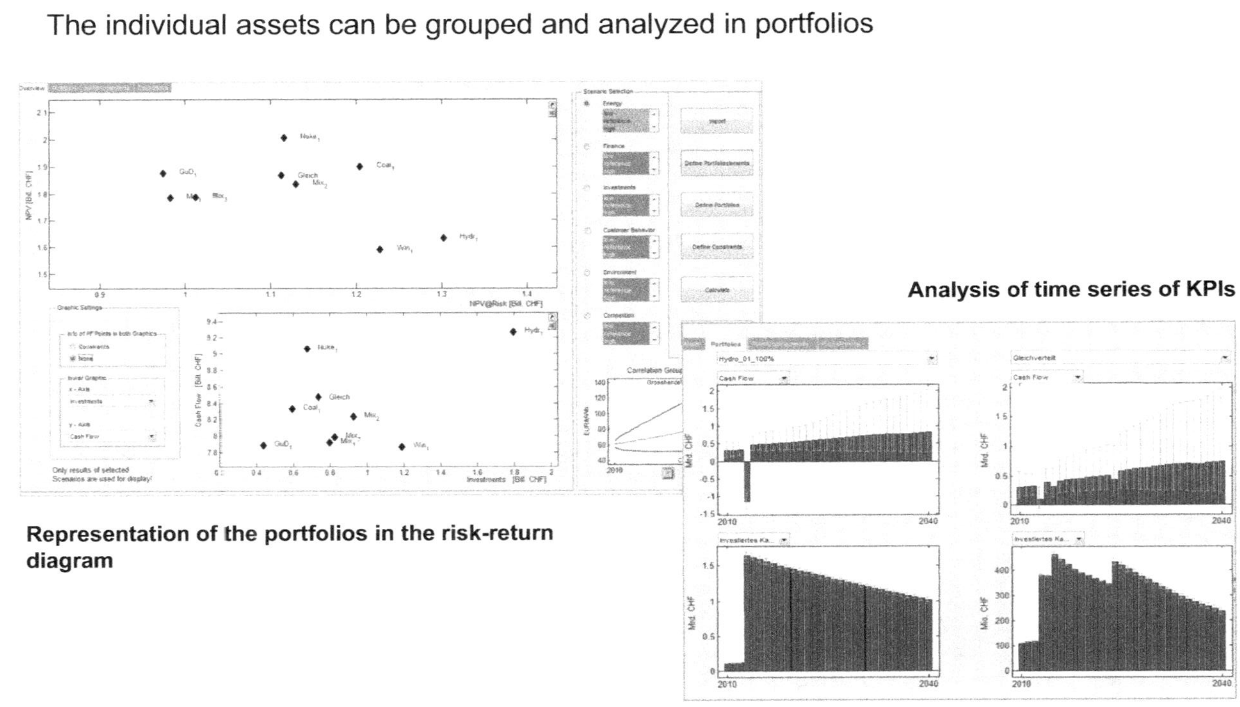

Appendix B: Tool to Support Scenario Analysis   177

Fig. B.3 Depiction of the results

References

Friedman, D. D. (1989). *The machinery of freedom: Guide to a radical capitalism.* Open Court Publishing Company.

Gebel, T. (2018). *Free Private Cities: Making governments compete for you.* Aquila Urbis.

Taghizadegan, R., & Otto, M. F. (2015). Praxeology of coercion: Catallactics vs. cratics. *Quarterly Journal of Austrian Economics, 18*(3), 294.

GPSR Compliance

The European Union's (EU) General Product Safety Regulation (GPSR) is a set of rules that requires consumer products to be safe and our obligations to ensure this.

If you have any concerns about our products, you can contact us on

ProductSafety@springernature.com

In case Publisher is established outside the EU, the EU authorized representative is:

Springer Nature Customer Service Center GmbH
Europaplatz 3
69115 Heidelberg, Germany

www.ingramcontent.com/pod-product-compliance
Lightning Source LLC
LaVergne TN
LVHW010959250326
834688LV00003B/16